D0015859

KAREN POND

GETTING GENKI IN JAPAN

The ADVENTURES and MISADVENTURES
of an AMERICAN FAMILY in TOKYO

Illustrations by
AKIKO SAITO

TUTTLE Publishing

Tokyo | Rutland, Vermont | Singapore

The Tuttle Story: "Books to Span the East and West"

Most people are surprised to learn that the world's largest publisher of books on Asia had its beginnings in the tiny American state of Vermont. The company's founder, Charles E. Tuttle, belonged to a New England family steeped in publishing. And his first love was naturally books— especially old and rare editions.

Immediately after WW II, serving in Tokyo under General Douglas MacArthur, Tuttle was tasked with reviving the Japanese publishing industry, and founded the Charles E. Tuttle Publishing Company, which thrives today as one of the world's leading independent publishers.

Though a westerner, Charles was hugely instrumental in bringing a knowledge of Japan and Asia to a world hungry for information about the East. By the time of his death in 1993, Tuttle had published over 6,000 books on Asian culture, history and art—a legacy honored by the Japanese emperor with the "Order of the Sacred Treasure", the highest tribute Japan can bestow upon a non-Japanese.

With a backlist of 1,500 titles, Tuttle Publishing is more active today as at any time in its past—inspired by Charles' core mission to publish fine books to span the East and West and provide a greater understanding of each.

Published by Tuttle Publishing, an imprint of Periplus Editions (HK) Ltd.

www.tuttlepublishing.com

Copyright © 2012 by Karen Pond
Illustrations Copyright © 2012 by Akiko Saito

Original versions of these stories were previously published in iNTOUCH, the monthly magazine of Tokyo American Club; and some also published in Tokyo Families Magazine.

Library of Congress Cataloging-in-Publication Data
Pond, Karen.
  Getting genki in Japan : the adventures and misadventures of an American family in Tokyo / Karen Pond.
    p. cm.
  "Original versions of these stories were previously published in iNTOUCH, the monthly magazine of Tokyo American Club and ... in Tokyo families magazine"--T.p. verso.
  ISBN 978-4-8053-1176-9 (hardcover)
  1. Pond, Karen. 2. Pond, Karen--Family. 3. Americans--Japan--Tokyo--Biography. 4. Tokyo (Japan)--Biography. 5. Tokyo (Japan)--Description and travel. 6. Tokyo (Japan)--Social life and customs. 7. Moving, Household--Japan--Tokyo. 8. Intercultural communication--Japan--Tokyo. 9. Maine--Emigration and immigration. 10. Japan--migration and immigration. I. Title.
  DS832.7.A6P66 2012
  952'.135051092--dc23
                                    2011031217

ISBN 978-4-8053-1176-9

Distributed by

North America, Latin America & Europe
Tuttle Publishing
364 Innovation Drive North Clarendon,
VT 05759-9436 U.S.A.
Tel: 1 (802) 773-8930; Fax: 1 (802) 773-6993
info@tuttlepublishing.com
www.tuttlepublishing.com

Japan
Tuttle Publishing
Yaekari Building 3rd Fl, 5-4-12 Osaki
Shinagawa-ku, Tokyo 141 0032, Japan.
Tel: 81 (3) 5437-0171; Fax: 81 (3) 5437-0755
sales@tuttle.co.jp
www.tuttle.co.jp

Asia Pacific
Berkeley Books Pte. Ltd.
61 Tai Seng Avenue #02-12, Singapore 534167.
Tel: (65) 6280-1330; Fax: (65) 6280-6290
inquiries@periplus.com.sg
www.periplus.com

14 13 12 11   5 4 3 2 1   1201TW

Printed in Singapore

For Bill, my husband and best friend.

At 2:46 PM on March 11, 2011, my family and I were in Tokyo when the frightening 9.0-magnitude Great Tohoku Earthquake struck. Within a few hours, I had heard from my husband and sons that they were safe and trying to return home. At 11:30 PM, the five of us were reunited in our Tokyo apartment.

However, our relief and joy in being together soon became horror as we learned of how the earthquake and tsunami had devastated cities in northeastern Japan.

Our thoughts immediately turned to the families and colleagues most affected by these twin tragedies; and also to the heroic workers at the stricken Fukushima Nuclear Plants.

This collection of stories is dedicated to Japan, our adopted home, which has had to bear the unbearable. We are once again amazed by your strength, sense of community and harmony in the face of such uncertainty. Japan is truly an amazing and extraordinary country.

Thank you for such memorable adventures. I look forward to many more together.

Table of Contents

CHAPTER *ICHI*:
clueless in japan

CHAPTER *NI*:
tokyo is not for the timid

CHAPTER *SAN*:
mama's getting genki

CHAPTER *ICHI*

clueless in japan

excuse me

I've started to say "Excuse Me." A lot.

A lot. A lot. A lot.

And, it's not because I've done something wrong or improper. I don't think so anyway. On the contrary, I'm finally, *finally* learning how to do something right.

It was just a week ago that my family—my husband, myself, three sons, one border collie, 11 suitcases, 36 tubes of our favorite toothpaste, a few Sudoku puzzles, numerous stir fry cookbooks and our fork collection—moved from Maine, USA to Tokyo, Japan.

"Well, boys," I said to my three sons as we were crowded together on our first Tokyo subway train. "Can you believe it? Just a few days ago we were in Maine. Now look at where we are." They nodded at me. "Seriously," I said again (trying to not sound too panicked), "Please look around. Where are we? Can you help Mommy? I really need you to help Mommy. We really need to figure out where we are."

It is at lost and confused times like these that I am extremely grateful our Tokyo Relocation Coordinator had already taught me the all-important, extremely-helpful, very-courteous, easy-to-pronounce Japanese phrase: *sumimasen* (soo-me-ma-sen). Of course, she also mentioned other crucial information, such as how to find my way home, how to thank someone for helping me find my way home, and how to use my new Japanese cell phone to call her when I couldn't find my way home. However, after an exhausting 24-hour journey across the globe which included traveling in rental car, shuttle bus, two planes, city bus and taxi, plus the 14-hour time difference, not to mention a tummy full of diet soda and airplane food, topped off with my high level of anxiety about moving to a country where we did not read or speak the language, I could process one thing and one thing only. And that was "sumimasen."

It was my first Japanese word. It meant "excuse me." I loved it.

"Sumimasen," I said to a fellow subway passenger as I tried to squeeze by him to get out the door. "Sumimasen," I said again as I accidentally and repeatedly stepped on his foot.

"Sumimasen," I said to the taxi driver later that afternoon when I fell out of the cleanest and most beautiful taxi I had ever seen. It was not my fault. I was mesmerized by the cleanliness. Not only was the taxi immaculate inside and out, but the driver wore an impressive blue uniform, complete with shiny cap and white gloves. Plus, in the back, the seats were decorated with most beautiful white lace doilies. This was not a public transportation vehicle, this was a mobile museum.

"Drive around the block on more time, please, and don't step on it," I said to the driver as I tried to think. After such an enjoyable taxi ride (The cleanliness! The professionalism! The white gloves!), I wanted to present the driver with a special thank you gift. But what?

I know. I know. Of course!

Clearly he appreciates the ornamental, so I will just quickly crochet another doily for the back seat. A heart-shaped one should do the trick. Perfect! Perfect! Perfect!

Not so perfect. Actually, on second thought, a doily may not be such a good idea after all. First, I don't have crochet needles. Second, I don't know how to crochet. Third, I am not artistic. My doily gift would probably look less like a heart and more like a droopy bottom.

I know. I know. Of course! Tipping. Perfect! Perfect! Perfect!

"Here's the fare," I said to the driver when we pulled up to the curb. "And, this is a tip for you."

"No tipping," he said as he graciously refused the money. He actually looked confused and a bit insulted.

Sumimasen.

Because I was so transfixed by the meticulous details of the taxi driver, his taxi and his refusal to accept a tip, I failed to notice that the passenger door had silently and *magically* opened. "One, two, three, ichi, ni, san," I said to the driver. With a smile and dramatic flourish, I gave the already-opened door a big birthing hip shove which immediately landed me on the curb.

Of course, the foreigner standing on the sidewalk was worse off than myself. He saw me in a very unladylike posture.

Sumimasen.

But, not even the taxi incident stopped me from continuing to use my first Japanese word.

"Sumimasen...chicken?" I said to the grocer the other day while grocery shopping.

"Sumimasen...Wii game?" I said to a clerk while trying to find a birthday gift.

"Sumimasen...starch?" I mentioned when dropping off dry cleaning.

"Sumimasen...shoes?" I asked the woman at the store. "USA 8 ½ medium? Cushioned insole?"

"Sumimasen...goodnight," I said to my son as I tucked him into bed.

"Dad!" my son yelled. "Mom called me Sumimasen again. C'mon, Mom. My name isn't Sumimasen. It's Ed."

Maybe, just maybe, I might be a bit too enthusiastic about my first Japanese word.

sticker shock

I stared at the uniformed pizza deliveryman in my doorway.

He stared at me.

"Some-very-fast-words-I-don't-understand-and-then-even-faster-words en desu," the deliveryman said again.

I stared at my son.

He stared at me.

"What did he say?" my son whispered.

"I'm not quite sure," I quietly said. "But I think it was way, way, way too long to be the price of the pizza."

I stared at the pizza deliveryman.

He stared at me.

Just as I was thinking of complimenting him on his company helmet and delivery scooter, he bowed and passed me a small piece of paper.

"*Reshito*," he said.

"Wow," I said as I reviewed the receipt. "Wow. Wow. And, wow."

And, there it was: my first receipt in Tokyo. We had been here for one week and I had never seen so many zeros. "Wow, wow, wow," I repeated, looking at the price again. "There are a lot of zeros here. Look! And, a comma too." My husband and I had thought that ordering pizza in would be "easy." Instead, I found myself in an international stare-off.

I stared at the very patient pizza deliveryman again.

He stared at me.

"Perchance, is this a decorative comma?" I asked. "You know, like not a *real* comma, but just one for ornamental purposes? And how about these zeroes? How about we turn one into a smiley face instead? There we go. It is a much friendlier number now."

In America 5,000 is a very big number, not to mention, a very, very, *very* expensive pizza. I gulped.

"Honey," I yelled down the hallway to my husband. "Did you order pizzas or buy the whole pizza franchise?"

I examined the paper in my hand once more. Maybe, just maybe, in my jet lagged state, I was seeing things.

Nope, I wasn't seeing things.

Yep, all three zeros were still there.

Yep, as we recently discovered, Japan is a cash-based society.

Nope, the emergency credit card was no good.

Yep, I needed yen. I needed lots and lots of Japanese yen.

"Quick!" I ordered my sons. "Check under the sofa cushions for some loose change!"

"But, Mom," my sons said. "We just moved in, remember? There won't be any money under the sofa cushions."

"You're right, you're right," I said. "Quick, go introduce yourself to our new neighbors and see if you can sell them our sofa."

"I feel good, really good," I said later between mouthfuls of pizza. Yeah, there was bit of a stumble with the cost, but I problem solved. Yeah, it wasn't as easy as I had thought it would be, but I still did it. I ordered a pizza in Japan and, not only that, I ordered a pizza my family liked (I somehow avoided the mayonnaise, tuna and corn special). Pepperoni pizza had never tasted so delicious! "I feel like a lioness that has brought back an antelope for the pride."

"OK, Lioness," my husband said. "Next time you are out hunting and gathering. Please be sure to find us a new living room sofa."

fire queen

Back in America, my weekly grocery shopping routine usually went something like this:

1. Sunday: drive minivan to the supermarket. Fill up shopping cart with items from aisles 2-10. Drive home with food.
2. Sunday through Thursday: eat the groceries.
3. Friday: (hopefully) go out to dinner or order take out.
4. Saturday: pick through leftover peanut butter sandwiches, pot roast and pie crusts or coincidentally walk by a neighbor's home around dinner time and hope to get invited to their barbecue.
5. Sunday: lather, rinse, repeat.

But, in Tokyo, it's a very different story. First, without a car, I can only buy as much food as I can carry or bike home. Second, completely illiterate of Japanese, I now must rely on my ability to interpret product labels.

"I am not sure," I said to my husband as I studied the picture on a package. "It could be a mini deodorant stick. It also could be an over-sized glue stick."

"And this," I whispered as I studied a cute, small pink box with a picture of mini rolled items. "It could be a box of sweets. But, then again, it also could be a box of sanitary products."

"Maybe we should try the meat cooler first," my husband suggested.

I put down the box of sweets. "Good idea. We should be able to figure out meat, right?"

Wrong.

Meat is packaged in small 200 gram portions. Metric meat is also very thinly sliced. It also costs over 200 yen per 100 grams. And we have three sons at home. Three very hungry sons.

1. How many thin slices of Metric Meat do you need to be able to smoosh together to make a hamburger patty?
2. How much can you buy with 2000 yen?
3. If one train leaves the station at 9 AM going 45 mph carrying a bushel of apples and the other train leaves station B at 11:30 going 60 miles per hour....

"Honey," I said to my husband in a panic. "I feel like I'm taking the aptitude test to get into college. Do you happen to have a no. 2 pencil and a graphing calculator?"

My husband, who scored very well on his aptitude tests, finished the shopping.

The next day I was on my own, but I was better prepared. I headed to the local store armed with critical shopping tools: lots of yen, a calculator, a Japanese/English dictionary, some pump-up music on my iPod, and a plan. My plan was simple and straightforward: to avoid becoming overwhelmed and intimidated, I would simply buy anything—*any bottle, any jar, any box*—that had English written on it.

"Hey, Mom," my son said when I came home from the store. "What's for dinner?"

I held up two items. Each had bold English labels on their packages.

"We're having TACO KIT and we're drinking POCARI SWEAT."

I followed the same strategy the next day.

"Hey, Mom," my son said when he came home from school. "What's for dinner?"

"Dinner," I answered as I held up the box. There was some Japanese writing, an adorable illustration of peppers and the English word DINNER written across the front of the box. "For dinner, we are having DINNER."

Now that I think about it (and after our tongues have properly healed and our swollen lips returned to normal), I probably should have paid less attention to the English and more attention to the red pepper drawing. DINNER turned out to be very, very, *very* spicy curry.

"Mom," my son said after his first bite. "DINNER stings! Oh God! DINNER is hurting me! I don't care who Pocari is and why we have a bottle of his sweat, but pass me the SWEAT! Give me the SWEAT!"

"Until you figure out the food, you might want to try shopping at an international market," my neighbor suggested after I explained what happened and repeatedly apologized for any loud crying and cursing from our apartment. "The international market is about 45 minutes from here, and it is more expensive, but the Japanese labels are translated to English. And, the store offers home delivery." Bingo.

"Thirty minutes," the check out clerk at the international market said after he boxed up my groceries. "We will be at your home in 30 minutes."

"How about an hour?" I negotiated. "It will take me 45 minutes to get home by subway or taxi."

"Thirty minutes," he repeated.

Because I was so excited to have found the store and familiar food, I completely forgot to ask about delivery times *before* I purchased the groceries.

If it takes me longer to get home, how am I going to be home first to accept the groceries?

"Excuse me," I asked in my sweetest voice. "How about if I ride with you *and* my groceries? We are going to the same address after all. I promise I won't touch the radio tuner."

"Thirty minutes," he repeated.

He bowed and walked off to help another customer.

I bowed and ran.

There was no time to waste. I had exactly 28 minutes to make it home. I did not want another dinner disaster. I needed this food.

So, I ran and ran and ran.

I ran down the escalator and up the hill. I ran to the subway station and to my connecting train. I ran past signs that said "No Running." I ran out of the train, up the station stairs and down two city blocks. I ran up the stairs to my apartment and then ran right into my neighbor.

"I did it..." I said in between breaths. "I...just...outran...the...delivery truck. I was nervous that I wouldn't make it, but I did...I did it."

"Oh," my neighbor said as she patted me on the back. "I guess I should have told you—you can ask the apartment manager to accept deliveries on your behalf. You personally don't have to be here."

"Right," I said as I massaged my shin splits. "The apartment manager, of course. I should have thought of that. By the way, do you have any smelling salts...or Pocari Sweat? I feel proud of myself and also a bit faint...."

the goal

My goal for this week: try to speak Japanese to someone other than my Sensei. Now, I adore my Japanese teacher. She is extremely well-mannered. And, she is very, very friendly. In fact, her favorite hobby seems to be introducing herself to strangers on the subway. She also enjoys telling the time. And, she is quite observant of the weather. Unfortunately, since she's my Japanese 1 CD Sensei, she's not much of a coffee drinker and I'm looking for a coffee-drinking friend.

I also decided that, starting today, I would try to speak Japanese using more than just the few reliable words of the past few weeks (*sumimasen/* excuse me; *ohiyo gozaimasu/*good morning; *konnichiwa/*good afternoon; *konbanwa/*good night; *arigato gozaimasu/*thank you very much; and *yosashi tora/*easy tiger—long story).

I decided to practice my new Japanese sentences at a local coffee shop. What could be easier than ordering a cup of coffee?

"*Eigo ga wakarimasu ka?*" (Do you understand English?) I asked the young man at the counter.

Silence.

"*Eigo ga wakarimasu ka?*" (a much less-confident "Do you understand English?")

More silence.

Clearly, something was not right. This is THE conversation starter that my CD Sensei uses all the time and she's never ever had to wait this long for a reply. In fact, by this time, CD Sensei and her new chatty friends have already discussed the time, remarked on the weather and figured out the opening hours of the bank.

"What?" the Japanese clerk asked me in English. "I am sorry, but I don't understand anything that you said. What language are you speaking?" He leaned forward and slowly asked, "Do...you...understand...English?"

I quietly nodded that I understood English. But thought it was best to pretend that English was not my first language. "Café au lait," I said with a bit of a faux French accent. "Beaucoup strong cafè. Oui. Oui. Merci beaucoup, monsieur. À la...la la...la...la."

Starting now, my goal for this week: find a new goal and a new coffee shop. À la...la la... la...la.

what did I say?

For a parent in a foreign country, the hub for information, resources and tips is clearly the school bus stop.

"Hair Maker?" a Bus Stop Mom repeated back to me.

"Yes, you know, a hair stylist," I explained. Beauty salons in Japan are called "Hair & Make" so I assumed the stylist would be called a Hair Maker.

"This place?" my teenage son asked me with surprise. "This place? Mom, c'mon! Don't you love me?"

"Listen," I explained. "I only heard about two places from the BSMs. This place offers the best deal in town."

"But, Mom," my son said. "I'm going to my first middle school dance at my new school. I can't get my hair cut here. Where's Dad? Daaaaaaad!"

We went to the more expensive Hair & Make shop down the street.

"Mom," my 10 year-old son said as he watched his older brother enjoy his first hair cut in Tokyo. "You didn't tell me that in Tokyo a hair cut comes with warm neck towel and a back massage! A hair cut, warm towel *and* a massage! This place ROCKS!"

"And you know what," he continued. "Now that I think about it, my hair is quite long. The bangs are just ridiculous. Can you please sign me up for a trim? Right now?"

"*Sumimasen!*" I said to the stylist as I pointed to my 10 year-old's head. "*Sashimi o kudasai.*"

Well done, girl, I said to myself as I proudly sat back down. You are really tackling Tokyo now!

First, you got out of the comfort zone, introduced yourself to new people and asked for a salon recommendation.

Then, you studied the route to the Hair & Make; fortunately found one that the boys liked; remembered to bring yen; and memorized enough Japanese phrases to communicate needs. Girl, you are too good. Too good.

Wait a minute.

Wait a minute.

"*Sumimasen! Skoshi! Skoshi!*" I said to the woman stylist. "I meant to say *Skoshi*. Little. Little trim." I was afraid to ask what I had requested a few minutes earlier. What did I say? What did I ask for?

I meant to ask for a little trim. Instead I mistakenly communicated for the stylist to shampoo my son's hair with raw seafood.

In Tokyo, Hair Makers can cut, shampoo, perm, color and massage, but, unfortunately, they can not make an embarrassed foreign mother disappear.

the depaato

"Take off your shoes! TAKE OFF YOUR SHOES!"

Today was my first outing downtown by myself. With my boys attending their new school and my husband at his new job, I was now on my own. It was time to start my Tokyo experience. Today, I decided to check out the *depaato*, a department store. Clearly, my first step was a misstep.

I checked my watch. Congratulations to me: a new world record. Up to this point, it had been taking me a few minutes to commit a cultural faux pas. This time, it was exactly two seconds.

"*Irashaimase! IRASHAIMASE!*" the smiling saleswoman chirped at me.

"Ira what?" I stammered. "I'm sorry. I don't understand. Is it the shoes? Do I need to take off my shoes?" Just a few days earlier at my first Japanese class, I mistakenly wore my outdoor shoes inside my teacher's house. I had absolutely no idea that I was supposed to change into house slippers. Perhaps my new teacher would have overlooked this initial mistake. But, then I mistakenly wore the house slippers into the toilet room; I had absolutely no idea I was supposed to change again into specific toilet footwear. After a confusing and somewhat embarrassing conversation of slipper etiquette, I figured the best way to avoid offending my teacher and humiliating myself even worse would be to forgo the slippers altogether. "*Sayonara, Sensei.* See you Thursday," I said to my bewildered Japanese teacher as I somersaulted from the rest room, down the hallway and out her front door.

I'm pretty sure it was at this point that my teacher increased my class fee.

Today, I was NOT going to experience another slipper slip up. So, I respectfully and politely took off my shoes at the doorway of the department store.

"*Irashaimase!*" the energetic saleswoman repeated.

"Thanks for telling me," I replied. "I got it now: no shoes."

"*Irashaimase,*" another saleswoman squealed at me.

"Yes," I said to her as I nodded my head. "I have taken off my shoes. I got the message."

"*Irashaimase,*" another saleswoman yelled from across the floor.

"Wow. You too? From way over there in the cosmetics section?" I said as I held up my flats for all to see. "All set now, ladies. No need to tell me again. My shoes are off. Now I know: *irashaimase* means no shoes."

Irashaimase, however, does not mean "no shoes." I surmised this on the second floor when two salespeople quickly approached me at the top of the escalator.

"IRASHAIMASE!" they said together in a very cheerful sing-song way.

"IRASHAIMASE!" more salespeople on the floor repeated.

Clearly, my initial interpretation was not correct. It does not mean "no shoes." So, what does it mean? Why is everybody saying it? What am I supposed to do? Maybe I walked in on a Japanese game show? Is this some sort of department store musical? Is today Happy Irashaimase Day? I quickly tried to think of other logical interpretation possibilities:

Irashaimase! IRASHAIMASE! Your pants zipper is down! YOUR ZIPPER IS DOWN!

Irashaimase! IRASHAIMASE! You don't wear white after Labor Day! NO WHITE CLOTHES AFTER LABOR DAY!

Irashaimase! IRASHAIMASE! Don't look now, but Brad Pitt is behind you! BRAD PITT IS BEHIND YOU!

Irashaimase! IRASHAIMASE! You have spinach in your teeth. SPINACH IN YOUR TEETH!

"Irashaimase means 'welcome'," my Japanese teacher patiently explained to me at my next language class. "They are welcoming you to their store."

"What do I say back?" I asked.

"You don't have to say anything."

"Are you sure it doesn't mean anything about Brad Pitt?"

I'm pretty sure it was at this point that my teacher increased my class fee once again.

Starting today, whenever I am greeted with *irashaimase*, I will offer a polite bow of thanks and then walk around confidently with my head held high, my teeth spinach-free and my shoes on.

While living in Japan, I might be clueless, but I certainly will not be clueless and shoeless.

foreigner faux pas

Today I met my first Japanese doctor.

I bowed.

He bowed.

I am good at bowing now. Bowing I can do.

And, after a several weeks of Tokyo living under my belt, I have become very good at pantomiming. I call it my survival pantomime.

"Hot," I said as I placed my right hand up to my forehead. I fanned myself with my left hand.

"Bad," I said as I pointed to my throat and then theatrically coughed.

"Duke," my doctor said as he pointed to the framed Duke University School of Medicine degree on the wall. He was educated in the United States. He can speak English. Got it.

I probably should have seen the degree. But I was not looking at the wall. I was looking at my doctor's long white lab coat. The English word "doctor" was embroidered on the pocket.

"Once I feel better," I whispered. "I think I might embroider my coat pocket with my achievement. My pocket embroidery would read: 3 births, 1 eyebrow."

My doctor is a serious man. No jokes. Got it.

My doctor also wears slippers in the office. Back home in the States, if a medical professional greeted me in slippers, I'm pretty sure I would have left the clinic rather quickly. But in Japan, slippers are a sign of respect. And, at this medical clinic, the doctors, nurses, delivery people and patients are supposed to wear slippers around the office.

Unfortunately, as I have now discovered, patients with 8 ½ wide American feet don't fit in the petite complimentary office slippers. So, big footed, one-eyebrowed patients like myself must walk around in their own socks. Their worn-out, threadbare, inappropriate, I'm-not-feeling-well-enough-for-clean-laundry socks.

Another foreigner faux pas.

So, here I sit in front of my new doctor. I'm trying to act as poised and sophisticated as possible, but it's quite difficult. My throat is throbbing, my body is aching and my non-pedicured tootsies are peeking out the numerous hosiery holes. This little piggy went to the doctor...this little piggy studied at Duke...this little piggy had socks...this little piggy had none...

"Any questions?" my doctor asked after the diagnosis of strep throat.

"Yes," I said. "Two questions: one, where do I pick up my prescription for penicillin?" I attempted to clear my throat.

"And two—more importantly—I just moved to town and realized that western-size footwear is really hard to find." I cleared my throat again and continued. "I could not help but notice your slippers. Do you think you could order me a pair of ladies Duke University slippers in 8 ½ wide? Please? Go Blue Devils...Rah...Rah...Rah."

you can't get there from here

At first glance, I knew I would never drive a car in Tokyo. It was not the city noise that bothered me. In fact, Tokyo is surprisingly silent—no beeping, no honking, no shouting, no cursing. But, I knew that if there was one driver who would destroy this zen and ruin the culture of courtesy, it would be me. To me, the city was an exciting yet bewildering web of side streets, nameless roads, noodle shops, fruit stands, bikers, walkers, strollers and scooters. Mathematicians may enjoy this navigation challenge, but English majors like myself, who prefer people watching and daydreaming, should stay off the road and in the coffee shop. Attach wire baskets to the front and back of my bike for groceries? Sure! Order special cushioned shoes for city walking? Sure! Get behind the wheel of a car in Tokyo? Never.

"Oh, don't be such a wuss," my new friend said to me. "Jump in and I will show you how easy it is to drive here."

"That's OK," I said. "It's just a 30-minute commute by subway."

"With the car," she said as she jingled her keys, "it will be a quick 10. I promise you."

"You have arrived at your destination," the navigational system repeated in English.

My friend and I looked out our respective windows. No, this was not our destination. Not even close.

"How long have we been driving?" I asked my friend Muffin* (*name changed to protect the newly licensed).

"I think about two hours," she whispered back.

"Do you think," I said as I looked down an unfamiliar area. "Do you think we are still in Japan?"

"We 'd better check our purses for provisions," my friend said. "We may need to spend the night in the car. Don't worry. Everything looks brighter in the morning."

I looked sternly at the GPS. I used my best Angry Mom Eyebrow Stare. "C'mon, Beverly," I pleaded. "Don't give up on us." (About 45 minutes ago, Muffin and I decided that our driving luck may change if we "named" the GPS. We chose the name "Beverly" because we both agreed that Beverlys are patient, reliable, and helpful.)

"C'mon, Bev," I said again. "We know we didn't follow your directions exactly. We know we made you recalculate the route numerous times. Please, Bev, now we are really lost. Please show us the way. Show us *any* way."

"You have arrived at your destination," Beverly repeated.

"Wow, Beverly," I said. "For having such a sweet sexy voice, you've got a stone cold heart."

It was at this point, as we continued to aimlessly drive around the city (and continually push the "calculate route" button) that I imagined a new kind of navigation system—one deliberately designed for those new to Tokyo, new to driving, or just a knucklehead like myself.

My new system would identify the driver as soon as the seat was adjusted. "Oh, hello there, Yummy Mummy (Yes, I would program my GPS to refer to me as Yummy Mummy). Giving driving another go, are we? My calculation determines 87% chance of getting lost. First stop: petrol station. We both know today could be a very *long* day."

If asked to recalculate the route 10 times, my new system would automatically acknowledge the real-time tension in the car and offer a solution. "System senses high frustration level. Original route aborted. Coffee shop route initiated. Turn left in 10 meters. Your favorite latte and a newspaper will be waiting for you. "

If asked to recalculate more than 10 times, my new GPS system would immediately initiate crisis mode. "Emergency measures initiated. Auto pilot on. Soothing music on. Massage chair on. Babysitter called. Dinner reservations made. Relaxing night out recommended. But, please, please, for goodness sake, this time listen to Beverly and TAKE THE DARN TRAIN!"

kore wa nan desu ka?

It must be a hand towel, I tried to convince myself as I studied the fabric again. It's got to be, right? As I have observed since moving here, most Japanese restaurants present customers with small, warm towels to wash their hands before eating. So, a hand towel definitely makes sense.

But this is an apparel shop not a restaurant. And, this towel is large. This towel is dry. And, this towel has a mysterious large pocket.

It's probably not a hand towel.

It must be a puppet, I tried to convince myself. It must be, right? Japan is a very courteous, quiet and respectful country. So, a little hand puppet makes sense. That way, you can quietly and courteously wave above the dressing room curtain for assistance.

It's probably not a puppet.

Usually, at this point during cultural confusion, I would perform my perfected "Sumimasen-and-shrug-routine" and hope someone would help me. Or, I would just look hopelessly confused and hope someone would help me. But, not this time. This time I am in a dressing room—my first dressing room experience. And, I've been in here awhile now, so I'm a bit embarrassed.

And, not to mention, I'm naked.

Maybe I could just use my cell phone to call the saleswoman outside my dressing room? But, what would I say? "*Konnichiwa, shujin wa salaryman desu.* (Good afternoon, my husband is a salaryman. [One of my recently-learned Japanese sentences]). I'm calling from Dressing Room ichi. What do I do with this white towel thing? What is it? *Kore wa nan desu ka?*"

I studied the non-towel, non-puppet again.

Got it. It must be a "gift." Of course. It MUST be. It's quite common in Tokyo for stores and restaurants to offer a "thank you gift" for your business. In fact, in the last few months, I've received a complimentary scoop of cherry blossom gelato, a small tote and several cute cell phone straps. But, why would the saleswoman give a gift to me as I was walking *into* the dressing room?

I don't think it's a thank you gift.

I studied the non-towel, non-puppet, non-gift, white cloth with pocket one more time. I got it! I got it! I finally figured it out!

Hop.

Hop. Hop.

Hop. Hop. Hop.

Hop. Hop. Hop. Hop.

Ouch.

"Oh!" a friend of mine said later. "You are talking about the *make up hood*. You put it on your head before you try on new clothes to protect the clothes from make up stains."

"For your head?" I said incredulously. "For your head? Really? I thought it had to be some type of special dressing room slipper. I put my feet in it and hopped around the store. No wonder I kept falling over."

soy to the world

CHEW. CHEW. CHEW. CHEW. CHEW.

"Mmmmm," I said to my husband's colleague as I put another forkful of pea pods into my mouth. In the dim light of the restaurant, I couldn't identify anything on the table that I liked to eat, or, more truthfully, that I could successfully eat with chopsticks, except for the pea pods. This was my first company dinner and I did not want to embarrass myself. "Mmmmm," I said again as I rubbed my tummy.

CHEW. CHEW. CHEW. CHEW.

At first, I was extremely appreciative of the pea pods. As soon as my husband and I entered the restaurant, I quickly realized that I was the only spouse who had come to the company dinner. The only spouse. The pea pods could help me hide my anxiety.

CHEW. CHEW. CHEW. CHEW.

Also, I appreciated the pods because eating allowed me to successfully hide my lack of Japanese language skills. Instead of speaking, I just smiled. I excitedly nodded. I gave thumbs-up signs. I enthusiastically winked.

"You haven't flirted with me like this in years," my husband winked back. "I need to take you to company dinners more often. Easy tiger."

CHEW. CHEW. CHEW. CHEW. CHEW.

However, despite the benefits of eating the pods, I was now tired of them. Really tired. They were incredibly difficult to chew.

"Call *Guinness Book of Word Records*," I said to my husband from the side of my mouth. "There is no doubt that I am chewing the toughest pods on the planet."

CHEW. CHEW. CHEW. CHEW. CHEW.

"Excuse me…" one of my husband's colleagues said as he walked over to us. "We are curious about something. In Japan, we squeeze the edamame bean into the mouth like this. We would never eat the whole bean. It is very fascinating that in your culture you eat the whole bean."

CHEW. CHEW. CHEW. CHEW. CHEW.

GULP. GULP. GULP. GULP. GULP.

Eda what? A WHAT? Squeeze the beans out? Don't eat the bean? Edamame? This isn't a pea pod? THIS ISN'T A PEA POD? No wonder I've been chewing these things for hours. I was really beginning to think something was horribly wrong with my teeth.

I have my integrity. I have my pride. I will not be humiliated by a legume.

"Oh, that is fascinating, isn't it?" I said as I continued chewing. "This is exactly how I eat edamame in my area of the States. It's tradition, really. It is good for the character. Mmmmmm..."

CHEW. CHEW. CHEW. CHEW. CHEW. CHEW. CHEW. CHEW. CHEW. CHEW. CHEW....

soaking it in

I looked at the woman behind the desk.

She looked at me.

I looked at the little, little, tiny, tiny towel that she just handed me.

Chotto matte. Wait a minute! Wait a minute. This is not a bath towel. I know the English sign says "BATH TOWEL," but this is NOT a towel. A hand towel, maybe. A veil, maybe. An eye patch, maybe. But certainly *not* a bath towel.

I looked at the woman behind the desk. She looked at me.

"*Chiisai desu,*" (it's little) I said in Japanese.

She looked away from me.

I looked at my backpack.

I hope, I really hope that I packed my travel sewing kit. Certainly I did not want to offend any customs. But, maybe, just maybe, I could quickly sew 2 or 3 or 50 of these small traditional towels together and create one big cover-up, perfect for us bashful types. Or, I could make a toga. Or, a ghost costume.

I looked at the woman behind the desk.

She looked at me.

"It's my first time at an onsen," I stated.

Yep. Today, I was doing it. I was really doing it. I was determined. Today I would immerse myself in a Japan cultural favorite, the hot spring bath.

Yep. I was doing it. I was really doing it. Well, actually, I wasn't doing it quite yet. First, I needed to get over the fact that this women-only onsen was public. I would be soaking with strangers. And, second, this onsen had a bathing-suit-less custom.

"So, basically, what you are trying to tell me is," I whispered to the woman behind the desk. "I am supposed to leave my clothes *and* my inhibitions in the locker room?"

Nothing, absolutely nothing, was going to be between me and the hot spring bath except my lipstick. I reapplied my lipstick.

After a few anxious minutes, a cleansing shower, a nervous giggle and a very quick sprint to the outdoor bath, I did it. I entered into the most glorious, wonderful, extraordinary, picturesque, unbelievably rejuvenating onsen.

As I soaked, I regarded my fellow bathers in a new light. They were not strangers now. They were my sisters. We were a sisterhood. The Sisterhood of the Suitless. The Sisterhood of the Quick Sprint. The Sisterhood of the Not-So Embarrassed. The Sisterhood of the Tiny Towel. And, what do sisters do? Chat, right? Shouldn't we chit chat? Shouldn't we trade recipes? Shouldn't we *at least* share addresses for the annual holiday card?

I looked at the one other Westerner in the onsen. Hello, sister.

"So....?" I said out loud as I tried to think of something to say. What exactly do you talk about in an onsen? Clothes? Soup?

My new sister leaned closer to me. "Your towel..." she loudly whispered as she pointed to my towel that I had randomly placed on a rock beside the bath. "You're supposed to put the towel on top of your head to help keep you cool like this. You are definitely *not* supposed to put it on the rocks. That's a real no-no."

Some sisters are just know-it-alls.

Yep, I did it. I really did it. The bottom line of enjoying a Japanese onsen? Stand tall, walk proud, wear a towel dollop, and soak it all in.

tom

Thanksgiving in America may start with making lists, making phone calls, and convincing my brother-in-law to make his famous cranberry sauce, but in Tokyo, Thanksgiving starts with measuring tape.

"Honey," my husband asked me, "what are you doing?"

"I'm measuring the oven," I said. "Because *if* I find a store that sells turkeys and *if* I can successfully find this store and *if* I can find my way home again, the turkey better fit in the oven."

"Oh, thank goodness," he said with a sense of relief. "For a moment there, I thought you were going to measure us for signs of *metabo*." (In Japan, "metabo" is short for "metabolic syndrome" which is a scientific and polite way to say that you have said *sayonara* to your skinny jeans.)

So, with my measuring tape in hand, I headed out to track down a Thanksgiving turkey. In downtown Tokyo, you can find 200 gram packets of chicken. You can find delicious, thinly-sliced shabu shabu beef; you can find sushi, sashimi, squid, octopus balls (don't ask), eel, sake and rice wrapped in seaweed. You can find wasabi-flavored chocolate bars and $80 melons, but a 14-pound bird? Not a chance.

"I just heard," my American friend excitedly whispered to me over the phone, "I just heard that a store outside the city may have frozen turkeys. We have to go now before they are sold out!"

"Look! Look!" I screamed. Two trains and one taxi later, I had my head in the freezer and my elbows out to protect my find from other desperate parents. "Look! I found one! And, it will fit in my oven and it has a pop up button! A POP UP BUTTON." I nearly cried.

I proudly carried my Tom out of the store.

Then, 20 minutes later, I carried my Tom back to the store.

It really isn't in my personality to argue with the subway security guard. I mean he's got the law on his side, not to mention a spiffy uniform and baton. What do I have? Just a frozen bird and a bag of giblets. I admit I didn't really understand what he was saying to me (for all I know, he could have been saying "Wow! Well done! I am impressed. You found a turkey with a pop up button! A POP UP BUTTON!"), but I knew he was talking about the turkey and the train. My interpretation: he did not like the combination.

"Tom who?" my husband asked me the next morning. "Who's Tom and why are we waiting for him?"

"Tom the turkey," I explained. "I couldn't bring him on the train yesterday. A taxi ride home with the turkey would have been too expensive. So, I shipped him. Tom should be arriving around 9 a.m."

"What?" my son said as he entered the room. "We are having a house guest? No one tells me anything around here anymore. I hope he doesn't have to stay in my room."

In America, you may wait for the arrival of the cable guy. In Tokyo, it's turkey time.

As I waited for Tom's arrival, I reflected on what I was thankful for.

I'm very thankful I found a turkey for Thanksgiving in a foreign country.

I'm very thankful I burned many a metabo calorie on this search.

I'm very thankful for the pop-up button.

And, of course, I'm thankful that my family has become adventurous and will embrace new experiences. Because, come Christmas, I think I just might skip the ordeal of tracking down all the ingredients for the traditional American feast. I have much easier menu in mind:

I'm thinkin' a big bucket of fried chicken.

tongue-tied in tokyo

What could it be?

I quickly tried to think of some of the other complimentary gifts my husband and I have received from other Japanese shopkeepers since moving here.

I looked at the wrapped holiday package once again.

Definitely too heavy to be dishware. Probably not a tea cup.

Definitely too big to be any kind of accessory. Probably not a cell phone strap.

Definitely too bulky to be a promotional giveaway. Probably not a pack of tissues.

Definitely too lumpy to be a decoration. Probably not a flower calendar. Could it be a bag of potatoes? A pumpkin?

What could it be?

"*Gifto desu*," the Japanese chef said as he presented the package to us. "For you." He bowed. Then, he waited for our reaction.

This was one of our favorite local restaurants. It was a tiny shop just steps away from our apartment complex, up a steep staircase, and above a liquor store. We had walked by it hundreds of times before we got the courage to open the door and walk up the stairs. The staff spoke limited English, but the beef was unbelievably delicious. I didn't want to disappoint or offend the chef. But, I had absolutely no idea what "the gifto" was.

What could it be?

"Oh, thank you. Thank you very much," my husband said to the chef after a few awkward moments. "*Arigato gozaimashita.*"

Clearly my husband had figured it out. "Honey," he said to me. "We have received a gift...I do believe it is a gift of beef tongue."

And, for the first time in my life, I was tongue-tied.

"Maybe," I said to my husband later that evening as we both stared at the block of tongue now sitting on our kitchen counter. "Maybe it's too special to eat. Maybe I'm supposed to wrap it up in washi paper or something. Or maybe I'm supposed place it on our mantel next to our good china."

"No," he said as he looked over the tongue. "We definitely need to cook it. And we should find a recipe fast. We probably can't return to the restaurant until we've tried it. They will definitely want to know if we liked it."

So I have two new missions for this week. I've got until Saturday night to cook and serve a beef tongue dinner to my family. And, maybe even more importantly, I have to figure out the custom for beef tongue gift giving. What is the etiquette? Am I supposed to show up at the restaurant with an equally thoughtful present?

What could it be?

The chef's expertise is cooking. He gave us a gift of food.
I suppose I could write him something...hmmm.

A Beef Tongue Ode
Oh sweet, beefy t
You are not chicken, nor pork
I've got your tastebuds
But you have my heart, tonight
Be a tasty tongue
Be a slice of deliciousness
And, if not tasty
Someone pass me the sake

Co-co-aaaaaah!

"Yes! Cocoa!" I said to my youngest son through chattering teeth. "Look! Hot cocoa will warm us up!"

My son and I had spied a new small shop on our walk home from the grocery store. We were really hoping, praying really, to find a hot beverage to warm us up on this unusually chilly afternoon.

"Perfect!" I said to my son. "They have an English menu. Cocoa is on the menu. This will be easy."

My version: What I thought I was saying

"Cocoa," I said to the woman behind the counter.

"Hai," she answered. And, that is all she did. No bowing. No nodding. No scurrying into the kitchen to make the drinks.

A few moments later after no response or service, I tried again.

"Cocoa," I repeated a bit louder.

"Hai," she said again. However, this time instead of making the drinks, she looked around her shop and then just looked at me as if she expected me to say something else.

So, I did.

"Brrr," I said as I hugged myself and pantomimed being cold. "Brrr. Brrr. Brrr."

She looked at me a bit strangely.

"Cocoa," I said one more time. Then, out of desperation, I pointed to the menu board behind her.

After a few moments of reviewing the Japanese and English items, she pointed to the word "cocoa" on the board.

"Hai!" my son and I both said. Yes!

"So desu ne," she nodded. And, then she slowly said to me, "Co-co-aaaaah."

Co-co-ah? Co-co-aaaah? OK. If "co-co-ah" is the pronunciation in Japan for "cocoa," then what was I ordering? What did she think I was saying?

Her version: What she thought I was saying

"Koko," I said to the woman behind the counter. ("Here. This place right here. I am here.")

"Hai," she said. ("You got it. A bit obvious, but you are right. I agree: you are here.")

A few moments later I tried again.

"Koko," I repeated a bit louder. ("Here. I am still stubbornly standing here. Telling you that I'm here. In this place. In this spot. Saying it loudly, but not ordering any food or drink, just telling you that I am here.")

"Hai," she said again. ("I agree. You are still here.") However, instead of making the drinks (which she didn't know I was ordering), she just stood there and looked at me as if she expected me to say something else (which would make sense because I was at the counter). Unfortunately, I hadn't figured out my mistake yet, so instead I did this:

"Brrr," I said as I hugged myself and pantomimed being cold. "Brrrrrr. Brrr. Brrr."

She looked at me strangely. (No kidding.)

"Koko," I tried one more time. ("Here. Here. Here. Love the word. Could say it all day."). And, then (it's about time!) I pointed to the menu board behind her.

After a few moments of reviewing the menu, she pointed to "cocoa" on the board.

"Hai!" my son and I both said quite enthusiastically.

"So desu ne," she nodded as she viewed the menu board. And, then after figuring out what I was trying to order, she kindly tried to explain my pronunciation error, "Co-co-ah."

Aaaah.

It is times like these that I realize while living in Japan I should probably forgo the language classes and pursue non-speaking activities like drumming or flower arranging or napping.

the worst (and best) compliment

"Konnichiwa," I politely greeted the police officer in English as I entered the local police station. "Do you...understand English?"

"No," the policeman answered in English. (Aha! Trick question! So you do *understand* English!)

"Umm....well...let's see...my son found a woman's wallet down the street, over by the swings on the playground," I continued. Because I did not know enough Japanese to explain, I was hoping he could understand at least some of what I was saying.

I put the lost wallet on the counter and pushed it towards him
He placed Japanese paperwork on the counter and pushed it towards me.

"*Gomen nasai,*" I said (I'm sorry) as I looked over the form I couldn't read. "*Wakarimasen.*" (I don't understand).

Although I *didn't* understand what he was saying, I *did* understand I was supposed to stay in the police station. I did understand I was supposed to fill out the form. I did understand he wanted me to explain where we found

the wallet. And, I did understand my quick trip
to the store with my son was going to take much
longer.

"Weeeeee," I said as I pretended to swing.
"Weeeee! I love to swing. Schwinnggg!"

"Mom, what are you doing?" my son asked me.

"The nice policeman needs to know where we
found the wallet," I said as I pretended to climb
a ladder. "I don't know how to say *playground* in
Japanese, so I am acting it out instead...Oooh, Oh,
look at me! I can swing. I can climb the monkey
bars. I can be a fireman sliding down the pole..."
If only my coworkers in America could see me
now.

My American coworkers couldn't see me, but the
officer could. Clearly, he was very confused.
My son could see me and he was clearly
embarrassed.

After a few minutes of watching my pantomime
performance, the policeman cleared his throat.
"You a...dancer?"

A dancer? A dancer? That's strange. Why would he ever think I was a dancer? Does a dancer swing? Does a dancer slide down a pole?

Oh no. Oh no. Oh no. OH NO!

"No, no, no, no, NOOOOO!" I said as I vigorously shook my head. "You have completely misunderstood my moves. I am not an exotic dancer...

Oh goodness, no....Oh, heavens...I am actually kind of flattered that you thought that...but no....wait! Do you think I am asking you to put money in the wallet to see me dance? No. No. No, sir. Lost wallet. Lost wallet. This is not good. Let me just quickly phone a friend who speaks some Japanese and see if she will help straighten this out...."

"You know what, Mom," my son said when we finally left the police station some 30 very tense minutes later. "These things never happen when I go out with Dad."

ohmygosh-imas

"What are you doing?" my husband asked me the other night.

"I'm practicing how to bow very, very low," I mumbled from the living room carpet. "I'm pretty sure I am going to have to apologize to my sensei. And, I'm also pretty sure, yes, in fact, I know for sure: this carpet needs a good cleaning."

"Oh," he said. "I thought you were on one of your yoga fitness kicks again."

Tomorrow I return to my Japanese class. My first language class in a very long time. And, I am very nervous. Very, very, very nervous. I will have to admit to my sensei that I haven't been studying. And that's not all. I will also have to tell her that I have my -mas's all messed up. I just can't seem to keep the Japanese verbs straight. I can't remember if I'm coming or going, taking or drinking, eating or meeting. Nomimas, norimas, mimas, kaimas, kaerimas, ikimas, tabemas, aimas—OH MY GOSH-IMAS!

"And, that's not all," I said to my husband who happens to be a very diligent student, "I definitely, definitely have come down with a particle problem."

I looked back at my notebook to review my particle notes one more time.

When saying "also," I need to use "mo."

For possessives, that's a "no."

For "and", that's "to."

Drinking, eating, watching, use "o."

Buying a peach, that's *momo*.

Confusing *mo*, *no*, *to*, and *o*—now that's a no-no.

"Well," my American classmate whispered to me before our Japanese class started. "Don't feel so bad. At least, you know the difference between *kudamono* and *kodomo*. The other day I went to a new store for my groceries. Instead of asking the clerk where I could find the in-season fruit, I mistakenly asked where I could buy fresh children."

Ohmygosh-imas.

when in tokyo

"That is certainly a strange looking microwave," I said to my husband when we first toured our Tokyo apartment. "Why is it in the laundry room?" "Ummm...that is the dryer," my husband quietly said.
The dryer? That little box is the dryer?

In America, I was the owner of a quick, efficient, super-sized dryer. Once in awhile, it would randomly eat my husband's business socks, but that was the price to pay for warm, fluffy, unwrinkled load of clothes. Twice a week, I would throw, shove, push, ram, and jam clothes into the huge drum. "What are you trying to do?" my husband asked me one night when he saw me knee-deep in the dryer. "You aren't trying to stomp grapes to make wine again, are you?"

"Nope," I said as I crushed wet clothes under my toes. "Just making room for some bath towels. I know I can fit more in here."

"You can keep up, can't you little guy?" I said to my new mini dryer.

But, it truly couldn't.

So, as I have quickly learned, when in Tokyo, do as the Tokyoites do. Instead of battling the dryer and calling it names ("You are lazier than the ice tray!" "You are more frustrating than folding a fitted sheet!"), I followed the lead of my city neighbors. I went to the local hardware store and returned with an outdoor laundry line.

"There," I said after setting up the line and hanging up the clothes on my back porch. "All is well."

All was well except my timing. Unfortunately, I hung up my first line of clothes the night before a typhoon. The next morning I had to face this unpleasant truth plus my first-floor neighbor.

"Sorry to bother you," I said. "Quite a storm last night, eh? Funny story here...well...I believe the storm...you are going to laugh...blew my pajamas onto your back porch and...yeah...oopsie...those are my unmentionables on your barbecue grill..."

Even now with the laundry line and a drying rack, I still have trouble keeping up with the dirty laundry from my three active sons and our messy noodle eating. I constantly have clothes and sports gear drying outside and inside the apartment: on the kitchen stools, over the desk chair, on the dining table, over the sofa.

"What are you doing?" I asked my son the other afternoon.
"Dad said I could watch TV for half an hour."
"You know my TV rules," I scolded. "If you are watching TV, it must be for one hour and you must spread out your arms. You know I've got sweatshirts to dry," I said as I draped the hoodies over his shoulders. "Remember to rotate your arms every ten minutes or so. Now, where's the dog? I need him to help me air dry this cashmere sweater."

the hygiene office

I had my paperwork. I had my money. I had my train route. I had my map to the town office. What I didn't have was Japanese language skills. Although I know some Japanese phrases now, whenever I try to speak Japanese, well, I don't really sound like a citizen of the world. "Today shitake mushrooms delicious good-looking let's display enjoyment together I buy much. That is. OK?"

"Dog registration," I simply asked again in English. "The pet office?"

I also didn't have any deodorant. And, I was really beginning to perspire. I had been standing in front of this customer service desk for several minutes now trying to figure out where to go to officially register my dog.

I leaned closer to the woman behind the desk. "You know...woof. Woof. Woof." Normally I don't bark. I would never bark. And, I certainly would never pant. But, this was not a normal situation. I didn't want to come back again and start over. By barking, I was hoping these women would instantly understand that the bark meant I had registration paperwork for my dog and not that I needed a rabies shot.

"Hygiene office," one of the cheerful women said as leaned back away from me and pointed to the map of the office complex. "Here."

"You are right. I am so sorry about my body odor," I humbly apologized. "I must apologize. It's nerves. I wasn't sure how to get to this building by myself. But, I found it. Here I am. But, this building is bigger than I expected. And, now, I am not sure which office to go to. And, I have to turn in this paperwork today. And all the signs are in Japanese. I am studying Japanese, but I can't say much except things like 'This is a pen.' Oh, by the way, this is a pen. And, now I'm babbling...nervous babbling..."

"Hygiene office," the very pleasant woman repeated and then bowed.

"I know I probably should have a medical professional check on my perspiration," I continued. "But today is not the day. Today, I have to register my dog. But, if I can be honest with you, I don't really think this bad hygiene is all my fault. It is quite humid today. Anyway, just help me find the office for dog registration and then my odor and I will be on our way."

When she pleasantly suggested "Hygiene Office" to me once again, I decided it was best to follow her advice. Feeling and smelling like a failure, I followed the map up the stairs and down the hall to the Hygiene Office. I was hoping for a spray of perfume, a cold cloth and helpful worker who would show me the way to the pet registration office.

When I arrived at the Hygiene Office, however, I realized that the woman at the front desk wasn't commenting on my perspiration after all. She was correct: the dog registration office is called "The Hygiene Office." Who knew? Well, for one, the woman at the front desk.

"By the way," my friend said to me later after I shared my day's adventure, "I guess you didn't know....but Japan has its own animal sounds. Pigs here don't *oink oink*, they *buu buu*. Cats don't *meow meow*, they *nyaa nyaa*. Roosters don't *cock-a-doodle-doo*, they *kokekokko*."

"And, dogs?" I meekly asked as I recalled my earlier barking in the town office. "Please, please, please tell me that dogs in Japan *woof woof*."

"They *wan wan*," my friend said as she shook her head at me. "They *wan wan*."

the table wrangler

Yes, I have learned many new things since moving to Japan. The new language, for instance: in the last several months, I have spent a considerable amount of time trying to memorize and differentiate similarly-sounding subway lines, train stations, streets, and shops.

"It's *Akasaka*," I said to my husband.

"No," he said. "It's *Asakusa*."

"Really?" I said. "I thought that was *Arakawa*."

"No, that is the name of our apartment manager."

"Aaaaah!"

I have also spent significant amount of time learning the currency—the exchange rate between the dollar and yen; the best loyalty point card deals in town; not to mention, the pronunciation.

"Mom, where have you been?" my sons asked me last week.

"Well," I answered. "I went to the bank to get money and there was definitely some kind of, let's say, miscommunication. I asked for yon-sen and ended up naked in a hot spring bath. So, how was your day?"

I have also learned about new food, new traditions, new schools, new maps. Even after several months, there is still so much more to learn.

"Look!" I said to my son the other day at a crowded coffee shop, "There's an empty table! Aren't we in luck today?"

"Look," my son said as we sat down. "A woman left her purse, phone and ID on the table."

"Oh dear," I said. "You know what we are going to do? We'll just sit here and keep an eye on the belongings until the owner returns. No doubt she will be extremely grateful that we were here to protect her personal belongings. We will make sure that no one steals her stuff."

"By the way, Mom," my son said. "A lady is staring at us."

"Yes," I whispered quietly to my son. "That happens sometimes. You know that. Your mother has big feet in this country."

"Um, Mom," my son said again a few minutes later. "The lady with a tray of food is still standing behind you. And, you know what, Mom? She looks exactly like the picture on the ID card we are protecting from thieves."

"There's no doubt about it," my friend said later that night. "You blatantly stole her reserved table. Hadn't you noticed that people reserve tables with their personal belongings here?"

Reserve a table with a purse? An unattended purse? Unbelievable. Incredible.

"Well," my friend said. "Think of it this way—Tokyo has provided an opportunity for you to reinvent yourself. And, it looks like you have done that."

Yes, I thought I would change during our stay in Tokyo. Become more knowledgeable about Japan, yes. Become good at Japanese cooking, perhaps. Become an author, yes, hopefully. But, become a thief, never.

show time

I was feeling good. I was feeling confident.

Even though I had never attempted to purchase concert tickets before in Japan, I was feeling good.

I knew the location of the ticket office.

I knew the cost of the tickets.

I knew I had enough yen to pay for the tickets.

I knew the date of the show.

I knew the time of the show.

I knew how to say "green" in Japanese (*midori*).

I knew how to say "day" in Japanese (*hi*).

I knew exactly what to do.

And, I was feeling good. I was feeling confident.

"Don't worry," I assured my sons earlier that morning. "Mom's got it all figured out. You can count on me. No problem. This will be easy. Piece of cake! C'mon. Why do you still look worried? I will get you the concert tickets."

"*Midori no hi o kudasai,*" (Green Day, please) I ordered very confidently to the clerk behind the ticket counter.

And, then, yes, I silently congratulated myself and subtly patted myself on the shoulder for my successful communication. There is no doubt. I am definitely performing my celebratory dance moves tonight when I present these concert tickets to my sons. Who's your Mama?

"*Midori no hi o kudasai,*" I repeated a few moments later. I had watched the clerk shuffle through some papers on the counter. I had watched him consult with his coworkers. I had watched him scurry to the back room and then return. And, now I was watching him scan through his computer screen. I know my Japanese was correct. Where are the tickets?

"*Midori no hi o kudasai,*" I said again, with a little less certainty.

After a few more minutes of serious contemplating and making an inhaling whistling noise that did not boost my confidence at all, the clerk proudly presented me a flier to an upcoming show.

"Mom!" my teenager said when I returned home from the ticket office. "You were gone for hours! Did you get the tickets to Green Day?"

"Well," I said. "Let's see. The good news is that for my first time at the ticket office, it was mostly a successful mission. I went there for tickets and I have returned home with tickets. However, in hindsight, I should not have literally translated "green" and "day" into Japanese...."

"Mom, did you get tickets to Green Day?"

"Here's a bit of trivia for you. Did you know that there is actually a holiday in Japan called Green Day? It is a day devoted to the outdoors..."

"Mom, did you get tickets to Green Day?"

"And, here is something else I learned: the phrase *Midori no hi kudasai* will not help you at all to get tickets to the Green Day concert. But, it will help you get five tickets to a flower arranging class and I am pretty sure I signed us up to plant a tree. Who's your Mama?"

"Mom, did you...?"

"Yes!" I cheered as I started my victory dance that I had practiced all the way home. "Yes, I DID get tickets to the Green Day concert. Eventually, I just simply said *Green Day* in English and pointed to the band poster that was on the wall."

"Umm...why are you telling me this story, again?" my friend asked me as we were walking in Shibuya. "Do you want to come with me to the Tokyu Food Show or not?"

"Honestly, I just don't want to buy tickets again," I said. "Although it was successful, I really haven't quite recovered from my last attempt. It was a bit exhausting and embarrassing."

"You don't have to buy tickets to the Tokyu Food Show," my friend assured me. "You don't have to buy tickets. You don't have to dress up. It is simply a popular food court in the basement of the department store in Shibuya."

What now? A food court? A food court? The Tokyu Food Show is a food court?

Since moving here, I had always thought that the Tokyu Food Show was a fashion and food event sponsored by the Tokyu department store. I thought models would parade down a runway with platters of the latest, greatest, newest and tastiest Japanese food. And, I thought you had to buy tickets.

Maybe it was the word "show" in the name that confused me.

Maybe it was because Shibuya area is the hub of fashion and shopping.

Maybe it was because the show was named after a popular department store.

Or maybe it was just me. I should probably stop interpreting words so literally.

Who's your Mama?

CHAPTER *NI*

tokyo is not for the timid

the swimming cap quest

"Swimming cap?" I asked my youngest son.

"Swimming cap," he said.

"Swimming cap?" I asked again.

"Swimming cap," he repeated as he handed me a note from his elementary school P.E. teacher. "I need a cap for swimming class. By Friday."

Friday? Friday? Wait a minute. That's not enough time. That's only two days away! I don't know Tokyo well enough yet to locate a sports store. I don't know the Japanese language well enough yet to ask for a swimming cap. All I really know how to say is:

> 1. *Ame desu ne.* (It's a rainy day out, isn't it?)
> 2. *Otenki desu ne.* (It's a nice day out, isn't it?)
> 3. *Konnichiwa. Kore wa pen desu.* (Good afternoon. This is a pen.)

Oh, wait, I know a very easy solution.

"No. No. No. No way, Mom," my son said as he shook his head back and forth. "I know what you are thinking. No, I am NOT going to shave my head."

"Swimming cap?" I asked the well-dressed older woman behind the desk. "Do you sell swimming caps here?" I had spent the morning and afternoon on the swimming cap quest. During this mission, I had discovered shops with fresh sushi, cold soba, sweet potato ice cream and some snack called octopus balls, but no swimming cap. It was on my quiet walk home that I passed a Japanese high school with a swimming pool. A swimming pool! Caps must be here.

"Tokyo is not for the timid. Tokyo is not for the timid. Tokyo is not for the timid," I said to myself as I followed the signs for the swimming pool entrance and walked in. Buck up now, step out of your comfort zone and get that cap.

"Swimming cap?" I said in English.

"Slippers," the beautifully dressed older woman answered.

"Swimming cap?" I said again. I wasn't sure she heard me correctly the first time.

"Slippers," she said again.

"Swimming capo," I tried. I had recently heard from other international friends that adding an "o" sound to some English words may help with communication. I crossed my fingers that this trick worked.

"Slippers-o," she said to me.

Nope, it didn't work.

Tokyo is not for the timid. Tokyo is not for the timid. Tokyo is not for the timid. So, that is why I did it. With much dramatic flair and finesse, I acted out putting on a tight swimming cap and then began to pretend swim around the lobby. My back stroke is awful.

"Slippers," the woman said again. This time she acted out too. She pointed to her feet which were in slippers. Then she pointed to my feet which were still in my outdoor shoes. Then, she pointed to the basket of complimentary slippers by the door. Got it. Take two.

"Ticket?" I said.

"Ticket," she said.

"Ticket?" I said.

"Ticket," she said.

It took about 30 minutes, but the two of us were now downstairs in front of the swimming pool in matching small brown slippers. We were both staring at the ticket vending machine beside the locker room doors. Another puzzle to solve. Do I need to buy a ticket for the slippers? Do I need to buy a ticket to use the pool? I don't need a ticket. I need a cap. How do I explain that? What do I do?

I bought a ticket.

"Swimming cap!" I said enthusiastically as the woman handed me a swimming cap after I purchased the ticket. The cap was behind the desk the whole time. It was beautiful. It was blue. It was waterproof. It was for an adult.

"Child cap?" I meekly asked. "This cap fits an adult," I tried to explain. "Do you have swimming caps for children?"

An hour later I emerged from the school. I bought a ticket to swim with no intention to swim; I bought a cap for myself because I didn't know how to explain I only needed a kid's cap; I bought a kid's cap after a bit more pantomiming; I swam the back stroke around the lobby. And, now I was bowing backwards trying to leave the school despite the fact that the extremely polite woman and her even more polite friend kept pointing me to the direction of the pool. They had seen my back stroke; they knew I desperately needed lessons.

"Swimming cap," I said to my son.

"Swimming cap?" my son asked.

"Swimming cap," I said again as I gingerly displayed it in the middle of our dining room table. I was absolutely exhausted but extremely proud of my success. Tokyo is not for the timid.

"Hey, Mom," my fifth-grade son said a few minutes later. "By the way, I have a note from my teacher. I need a recorder for music class. By Friday."

a tokyo triumph

Think. Think. Think.

"C'mon," I encouraged myself in the mirror. "Think! Think! Think! You can figure this out!"

"Aren't you an educated, clever, confident, competent woman?" I asked myself.

"Yes, I am!" I confidently answered.

"Haven't you persuaded your sons to try new foods and eat with chopsticks?"

"Yes, I have!" I said.

"Haven't you triumphed over train schedules? Haven't you become proficient with the spaghetti-like network of Tokyo trains and subways?"

"Yes! Yes I have!" I cheered for myself.

"Haven't you moved across the globe? Haven't you met new friends? Haven't you tried to speak a new language? By golly, haven't you had the courage and self confidence to walk around in your glory to soak in an onsen?"

"Yes, I have! Yes, I have!"

"Then," I said to my reflection. "You can do it. You can figure out how to flush the toilet."

No, I can't. I really can't.

Yes, it's true. I have met my match with the public Japanese washlet. Believe me, I have tried every which way to flush and now I am simply out of ideas. I have never been so completely flustered. This is a new low.

Think! Think! Think!

Is there a wall button? To be honest, even if there was a wall button with the word "flush" written in bold English letters, I would never press it. I learned this lesson on Tokyo Day One at our apartment when I incorrectly assumed that the big red button on the panel near the toilet was the flush. It was not the flush. It was the emergency button. Flustered and embarrassed, I didn't have the heart to tell the security team that it was a false alarm, so I mumbled something about running out of two-ply.

Think! Think! Think!

Is there a handle? Is there a sensor? No and no. I have inspected the throne area for a handle. I have waved my hand around just in case there was an automatic sensor. I have even reached around the walls for some kind of pull chain. I am stalled. I have never, ever, *ever* spent so much time contemplating plumbing.

Think! Think! Think!

Maybe it's voice activated? "Done!" I said out loud. "Finished...Completed... Concluded...All set...Bye-bye...."

Nothing.

Stupid. Stupid. Stupid. Of course! This is Japan! If the flush is voice activated, it would not be in English. It would be in Japanese! I stared at the commode with my fingers crossed for luck, "SAYONARA!"

Nope. It's not voice activated.

Think. Think. Think.

Stomp. Stomp. Stomp.

What? A floor button! A FLOOR BUTTON! The button on the floor runs the water! You did it! You figured it out!

Take that, toilet. You may have intimidated me. You may have surprised me with your warm seat and startled me with the bidet spray. But you did not defeat me.

"Oh, that's right," I said to my reflection, "You are a competent, confident woman. You can do it. You can figure things out. You can triumph in Tokyo."

"You know what?" I said to my husband when I finally returned to the restaurant table. "Everything in Tokyo is new and foreign, but I am prevailing. I am succeeding. I am a new woman. I am confident, competent, problem-solving woman. That's right. I am Tokyo woman, hear me flush!"

"OK, Tokyo woman," my husband whispered to me. "Did you realize you just shuffled across the restaurant in the toilet slippers?"

the lab

Success!

"Honey," my husband asked me in the bread aisle. "What are you doing?"

"Who? Me?," I said. "Oh, I'm just...texting..."

"You took a picture of the Japanese cereal box, didn't you?"

OK. Yes. I admit it. For several months now, I have been on the lookout for a better strategy for successful grocery shopping at my local grocery store. For the most part, I can identify majority of the fruit and vegetables, but everything else still has me spinning in circles. Shopping mistakes still happen.

"Boys! Great news!" I said the other morning. "Mommy found danish! This is so exciting! Here, take a bite. Take a big bite."

"Mom," my son said with a mouthful of food, "my danish has beans in it! Beans! Why are you punishing me? Is it because I am taller than you now? Is it because I told someone your real age? Is it because I convinced you that you accidentally bought octopus genitalia soup? Whatever I did, Mom, I'm sorry. Believe me, I am really sorry."

But, now I have a new shopping strategy. Starting today, I am using the camera on my cell phone to take pictures of grocery store items. With these photos, I can record and file what my family likes and what my family doesn't like. I won't need to carry my Japanese and English dictionary with me to the store anymore. I won't have to pantomime anymore.

"Isn't that the milk the boys like?" my husband asked me as we surveyed the numerous cartons with a cow on the label. (A picture of a cow on the carton is the clue that it's a carton of milk. And, I followed the cow clue faithfully until the other day, when I brought home a cow carton that was not milk. It was a carton of thick drinkable yogurt.)

"Oh, right!" I said. "That's the one." Click!

I might not be able to read Japanese yet, but I can take a damn good photo. Click! Click!

"Work with me. Work with me," I said to the package of our favorite bread, snack pretzels, soba noodles and soy sauce. Click. Click. Click.

"Smile, Tony, smile," I said to the blue cereal box with the famous tiger. "I'm filing your photo under GREAT." Click.

"And, you," I said to the pastry-looking item. "You surprised me. You are not danish. You are some kind of bean-and pork-filled imposter bun. I won't make that mistake again." Click.

Yesterday, I was wandering the aisles looking confused, helpless and hungry. Today, on the contrary, I look like a multi-tasking gadget guru.

OK, yes, I admit it. My new strategy does make shopping easier. It does make shopping quicker. It does make shopping more successful. Unfortunately, it doesn't make me a better cook.

"Mom, what...is...this?" my son asked me as he stared at his dinner plate. "Well," I said as I also picked through my bowl. "It is *supposed to be* stew. I found all the ingredients, so I decided to use our slow cooker. Well, apparently, I forgot about the different voltage. Instead of four hours, I should have set it for four weeks. Here, wash it down with some drinkable yogurt."

Until I figure out shopping and cooking, another strategy is definitely in order.

"Boys," I said to my family, "you know that Mommy is trying her best. I am taking Japanese classes. I am memorizing Katakana. I have enrolled in Japanese cooking classes. I will only become friends with people who will give me a recipe. I have steamed labels off bottles to bring with me to the store so I will correctly match and purchase items that you like. I have followed Japanese mothers around the store to see what they buy. I have traveled 45 minutes to shop at the international supermarket. And, now I am inconspicuously taking photos with my phone. The point is, well, it is going to take more time. So, here's the deal: until I figure out food, please refer to the kitchen as *Mommy's Lab*; and, yes, I will pay for your patience. Everyone gets an extra 500 yen in their weekly allowance. Except your father. He gets an extra 1000 yen."

the old song and dance routine

Here we go again.

The last time I was at this grocery store I was looking for soba. A friend of mine had recommended this noodle. So, I wanted to try them for dinner. But first I had to find them.

"Excuse me. Can you please tell me where I can find soba noodles?" I asked the clerk. From the look on his face, I instantly knew that this would be a lost-in-aisle-six-translation moment. And, just before I started to pretend to slurp imaginary noodles, I simply asked: "Soba?"

"*Hai!*" The clerk answered. ("Hai" means "I understand" and you must understand how I understand how much I love hearing this word). He kindly showed me the soba and then curiously watched as I took out my phone to take a digital picture of the package.

And now here I am again.

"Frosting?" I asked the clerk. "Cupcake frosting? Cake frosting?" I had found cake mix and muffin tins, but I couldn't find the convenient cans of ready-made frosting.

"Frosting?" I asked again. "Icing?" I tried a synonym. "Sugar bomb?" This time, there was no "Hai" reply.

At times like these, I resort to my desperate communication method: the ol' song and dance routine. So, I pointed to the frosting on the cake on the cake mix box. I cleared my throat. I blew out imaginary candles. And I started to sing: "Happy birthday to you. Happy birthday to you..."

"No. No. No," the clerk said as he shook his head.

"I know. I'm sorry," I apologized. "I'm a terrible singer. We don't have talent in my family, but we do have enthusiasm."

"No," he said again as he pointed to the picture. "In Japan, there is no icing. We do not import icing."

What? No. No. No. NOOOOO! It's my son's birthday this week and he wants to share cupcakes with his classmates. What am I going to do?

The store did sell bags of icing sugar, however. So, after a bit of Internet researching, I was able to find a frosting recipe and a metric conversion table for the ingredients.

"You taste it," my youngest son said to his older brother as they looked over the tray of frosted cupcakes. "You're the oldest, you go first."

"No," my oldest son said. "It's your birthday. You have the first bite."

"Mom," my son said after the first taste. "It tastes right, but it looks wrong." He was right. I had never made metrically-converted homemade frosting before and it did look wrong. Maybe it was the different butter? The milk? The drinkable yogurt? My math? Maybe I am going to cry.

Tokyo is not for the timid. Tokyo is not for the timid. Tokyo is not for the timid.

"Sweetie," I said to my son. "Maybe, just maybe, with a little creativity, Mommy can fix these cupcakes and avoid a birthday dessert disaster."

And, that's why, if the elementary school principal calls, my son went to school today with birthday cupcakes completely covered in whipped cream and chocolate candies.

That's my story and I'm sticking to it.

fresh money

"What? Can you repeat that?" I said to a Japanese friend of mine. "What did you say?"

"The money," my friend said again. "The money must be clean. It must be fresh."

Fresh money? *Fresh money?* I don't understand. Is there actually sour money in Japan?

Recently, my husband and I were invited to our first Japanese wedding. In my attempt to avoid making any mistakes (or at least any obvious mistakes) at the ceremony, I asked my friend to teach me about Japanese wedding customs.

"As a guest, please wear a formal dress," she said. "And, your husband needs to wear a dark suit."

Got it. Easy.

"You need to say *omedetougozaimasu* (congratulations) to the wedding couple and their families," my friend suggested.

"Omedetougozaimasu," I repeated.

Got it. I can do that. Easy.

"You do not bring a present."

"Really?" I asked in disbelief. "Actually, I am relieved. I wasn't looking forward to running around Tokyo searching for blenders, matching salt and pepper shakers, or heart-shaped waffle irons."

"In Japan," my friend continued. "The wedding gift is cash. It is always cash. Please enclose the cash into the special festive wedding envelope."

Find special wedding envelope, I wrote in my notebook.

"Got it," I said. Still sounds easy.

"And," my friend said very seriously, "this is very important. This is critical. Please remember—the wedding gift money must be clean. It must be fresh. Otherwise it is bad luck."

Fresh money? *Fresh* money?

"Can you repeat that?" I said. "What did you say?"

"Fresh," she said. "No wrinkles. No creases. No folded corners."

It was at that point that we both noticed the clothes I was wearing—a wrinkled shirt, a creased skirt.

"Well, at least no folded corners…" I said as I tried to straighten my outfit. "I think," my friend suggested, "to be safe, I think you should iron the money."

Iron money? I can't iron money. First, I would be too nervous. Second, what happens if I burn it? If it is bad luck to present wrinkled money, it must be horrible to present charred, smoking yen.

I definitely need a professional to help me with this fresh money custom. I am certainly not going to do the ironing.

I got it.

"I already took care of it," I said to my husband when he asked me about the wedding money. "I figured out what to do."

"Great!" he said. "So, you took the wrinkled bills to the bank and exchanged it for wedding-appropriate money?"

"The bank?" I said. "Well, no, not quite, but that's a good idea for next time. I actually took the money to the dry cleaners."

"Here you go," I said to my dry cleaner earlier that morning. "Five men's business shirts. One suit jacket. One pair of men's trousers. One dress. And, 50,000 yen. Little starch, please. Definitely no wrinkles. See you Wednesday."

the test

You can do it, I said to myself. You can do it. Don't be timid. Be strong.

I bowed.

He bowed.

I looked around nervously.

He looked around nervously.

I gathered up my courage, cleared my throat and said in Japanese "*Konnichiwa.*"

"Konnichiwa," the pharmacist answered.

Some awkward time passed.

I gathered more courage and said, "*Hajimemashita. Doozo yoroshiku. O tenki des ne? Kore wa pen desu.*" (Nice to meet you. The weather is nice, don't you agree? This is a pen). OK, I admit it was a bit of a nervous rambling, but at least I said something.

The pharmacist looked around nervously.

I bowed.

He bowed.

I left.

You can do it, I said to myself. You can do it! Don't be timid. Be strong.
At the next pharmacy around the corner, I decided I would forget about the
pleasantries about the weather and pen, and, instead, just pin my hopes on
sumimasen, the word that works miracles in Japan.

"*Sumimasen,*" I said to the pharmacist, "*Stomach medicine ga arimas ka?*" I
pointed to my stomach. "*Heartburn desu. Stomacho ashido o motte imas.*"
Is that right? No, that's not right. What am I saying? I can't do it.

I looked around nervously.

Pharmacist #2 looked around nervously.

I bowed.

He bowed.

I left.

You can do it, I said to myself.

You can do it! Don't be timid. Be strong.

"Ooooooh," I said to the next pharmacist further up the narrow road. I could not go home empty handed. I will not go home empty-handed. I had promised my husband that I would find him some over- the-counter antacid. And, that is what I intended to do.

"Ooooooh," I said again as I pointed to my stomach. Then, I patted my stomach. Then, I rubbed my stomach. Then, I patted it again. Just for an extra dramatic touch, I touched my forehead to indicate that I wasn't feeling well.

"*Wakarimashita,*" (I understand) the pharmacist said as he wrapped up something for me. I didn't even pay attention to what he wrapped up. I was so thrilled, so overjoyed that I successfully communicated!

I did it! I did it! I really did it!

I didn't do it.

I did spend my morning at three pharmacies. I did try my best. But when my husband opened up the package, I realized I didn't bring home antacid medicine.

I had bought my husband a pregnancy test.

dear diary, part 1 & 2

Part 1

I am so excited. So excited! The other night I went to my friend's house for a birthday party. Not just an ordinary friend. My best friend in Tokyo.

"You are my best friend in Tokyo," she said as she hugged me. "It's so great to have found such great friend. I didn't know I was going to find such a great friend but here you are!"

I did it! I really did it! I am no longer friendless, I have found a true friend.

Oh no, it wasn't easy finding a friend in a foreign country. First, I had to remember how to find a friend. I actually think the last time I had to find a friend was in kindergarten and that was easy. Sit near the girl with all the crayons. Stay away from anyone who eats paste. Learn how to skip rope. Done. Done. Done. By afternoon snack, I had a best buddy.

But, here, in a foreign city, well...how exactly does an adult find friends? Where do you start?

For me, I started on the first floor of my apartment complex: the mail room.

"Oh, hi there," I said to the first person who entered the mail room to open

her mailbox, "What a coincidence! You caught me getting my mail, too. We both get mail. That's cool. We haven't met yet. I never do this, but would you like to go out for some coffee sometime?"

"Actually, I don't drink coffee," she said, "Thanks though. See you another time."

Open mailbox.

Close mailbox.

Peek around the corner of the mailroom.

Open mailbox.

Close mailbox.

Peek around the corner of the mailroom.

"Oh, hello there," I said to the next person who entered the room. "Just checking for my mail. You're here for mail too, right? I see we both like to check the mail....How about coffee? Do you like coffee? Would you like to join me for coffee sometime?"

"Oh, I'm busy this week," she said, "Perhaps some other time."

Open mailbox.

Close mailbox.

Peek around the corner.

Open.

Close.

Peek around the corner.

Open.

Close.

Watch the sun set.

"G'day," a woman said to me. I had fallen asleep while leaning against the mail room wall.

"Whatever," I said in a bored voice. "You wouldn't want to have coffee with me sometime I bet, right?"

"Coffee?" she answered in an Australian accent. "Honey, I don't drink coffee. But, I do drink beer. Why don't you come over now?"

Toss the confetti. Ring the bell. I found a friend.

I also tried to find more friends at my boys' school bus stop. The hard part was actually getting to the bus stop. My boys don't really need me to escort them anymore. "It's raining," I pleaded. "I'll carry the umbrella, if you let me walk with you."

"OK, Mom. Just this time. But no kisses at the stop, please. Discreet chin nods only."

But, as I now discovered, the best way to find a best friend is through the school activities. I met my best friend while cheering for our sons' football team.

"You are my best friend," my best friend repeated at her party. And, I took a picture of us. Me and my best friend.

It took some time, but I've got a buddy.

I am excited. So excited.

Part two
Scratch the last entry.

Yesterday on campus I saw my best friend, my amigo, my tomodachi, mon ami, my freund. "Hi!" I said. I air kissed her cheek. Best friends air kiss.

"It's too bad you didn't make it to my party last night," she said.

Apparently, I look like someone else altogether in the dim light, and after a few glasses of wine.

"Hey," my husband asked me. "Where are you going?"

"Home," I said. "I'm heading back to the mail room."

CHAPTER *SAN*

mama's getting genki

hey, mom, what's for dinner?

13,140.

According to my calculations, this is the number of times my sons have asked me,

"Hey, Mom, what's for dinner?"

And that number doesn't include the multiple queries that start at wake up and never let up until I give an acceptable and delicious-sounding answer. For some reason (most likely my famous flop of French onion soup) my kids always have to know the dinner plan. At one point, they wouldn't even get on the morning school bus without knowing what culinary adventure awaited them upon return. While other bus riders were happily listening to music or reading, my boys would have their panicked faces pressed against the window. As the bus pulled away, I would see my sons anxiously mouthing, "Mom, what's for dinner? Mom, what's for dinner? Please no soggy soup bread. No soggy soup bread...."

Clearly it was essential to get my boys and myself more excited and less frightened about dinnertime. Hence, theme nights.

"Hey, Mom, what's for dinner?"

"It's Meatloaf Monday!" I would enthusiastically cheer. "Give me an M! Now an E...."

"Hey, Mom, what's for dinner?"

"It's a bowl of soup for the Super Bowl!" I would excitedly answer. "Quick! I'm open. Pass the bread! Touchdown, Mom!"

"Hey, Mom, what's for dinner?"

"It's Leftober time," I eagerly explained. "Leftovers in October. Get it? Anyone? Anyone?"

And, then we moved to Japan.

And, I admit, due to my not-so-impressive culinary and language skills, I have had my share of challenging moments trying to figure out a meal that my family will like.

"Hey Mom what's for dinner?"

"It's Onitober time," I sang as I presented a tray of rice balls wrapped in seaweed. "Onigiri in October. Get it? Anyone? Anyone?"

How do chefs do it? How do they keep their diners happy on a consistent basis? How do they attract them to their dinner tables? How do they tempt the tastebuds? How do chefs convince diners to come in and sit down?

So, the other day, I went searching for solutions in "Kitchen Town," an area famous for its restaurant and kitchen supplies. After an afternoon strolling through Kappabashi-Dori contemplating new pottery dishes, bar stools, chef's costume and very impressive Japanese kitchen knives, I saw my solution. I got it. I got it. I got it.

"Hey, Mom," my son said as soon as he came home from school. "What's for dinner?"

"Take a look," I said as I escorted him back into the hallway.

"The dinner is inside the old aquarium?"

"This, My Dear, is not an old aquarium anymore. You know how Tokyo restaurants display plastic food models of their menu in front of their shops to entice customers? Well, now, Mommy is doing it too. In this aquarium...I mean...*display case*, you'll see plastic models of the meals I can prepare— there's spaghetti, fruit, pizza, stirfry, ice cream parfait, scrambled eggs and frothy beer. No more surprises. No more stress. No more theme nights. No more Leftobers. Simply peruse and choose. What you see is what you get...well, for the most part. The frothy beer is for me."

My homemade food may never get any compliments, but, let me tell you, my Japanese fake food, now that is definitely something to brag about.

fuzzy rice

I looked at it.

"So, what do you think?" my husband asked. (To be honest, when my husband called earlier and told me he was bringing home a "surprise," I wasn't really thinking cookware. I was thinking more along the lines of jewelry.)

"Well," I said as I looked over the new rice cooker. "For starters, it is definitely too big and heavy for me to wear on my finger."

So, here we go: another new experience in Japan. In my attempt to immerse myself into the Japanese culture, I have arranged flowers, sculpted pottery, slurped noodles and perfected eating with chopsticks. I have tried a new language, eaten new food and forced on a pair of tiny nylons (imagine my surprise when I finally wiggled them on and discovered there were painted tattoos on the ankles. "Daaad! Mom has a tat! Mom has an ankle tat!"). And now I am trying a new gadget.

I looked at the buttons.

"So, what do you think?" my husband asked as he also studied the panel.

"The bad news: no English manual," I said. "The good news: this cute rice cooker looks a lot like R2D2 from the *Star Wars* movies."

"Well," my husband said. "We might not be able to figure out how to cook rice. But it looks like we can get a holographic message from Princess Leia."

"The pressure's on, R2," I said to the cooker later that night, "You won't fail us, will you?" I am pretty sure it beeped back at me to please find Obi-Wan.

I looked at the empty cooker.

Then, I added some rice. I added some water.

I pressed the one English button. I closed the lid.

"Mom," my son asked me with surprise. "What are you doing?"

"Making rice," I said confidently as I patted cooker. "Isn't that right, R2?"

"No, Mom," he said. "According to this button you just pushed, you are making *fuzzy rice*."

I looked at the button again. He was right. The button was labeled "fuzzy" in English. Fuzzy rice? Fuzzy rice? Over the years, I have made all kinds of rice—mushy rice, one-minute rice, burnt rice. I have made long-grain, short-grain, brown, and jasmine rice. I could win a gold medal with soggy rice. But fuzzy? I'm a bit fuzzy on fuzzy.

Twenty minutes later, I peeked at it. Just in case, I also had a local take-out Indian restaurant on the phone; butter chicken was my backup dinner.

"It is perfectly cooked," my husband noticed.

"That was easy," I said.

If I have learned anything by living overseas so far, it is this: if something works well, you stick with it until your family threatens to strike.

So, move over, microwave. Put a lid on it, stove top pot. The rice cooker is now the center of attention.

Sorry, princess, you are on your own to fight the Empire. In my house, it's fuzzy cookin' time.

it's all in the cards

"Read it and weep," I said to my husband as I showed him my brand new loyalty card. "Can you beat the bookstore?"

"Two words," he said with confidence. "Bic Camera."

Oh! Trumped by that home electronics store again!

After several months now in Tokyo, my family and I have adopted some interesting Tokyo traditions:

We now eat with *hashi* (chopsticks). (Some of us are better than others.)

We can speak some Japanese. (Some of us are much better than others.)

We remember to take our shoes off at the door. (Some much, much better than others.)

We bow while talking on the phone. (OK, that was just me. And, it happened once.)

We sumo wrestle. (OK, that's just our youngest son and he won second place.)

And, now we have a *pointo caado* (store loyalty point card) collection.

Getting a pointo caado is easy as *ichi, ni, san.*

1. The clerk of any store: "Fastjapaneseyoucan'tunderstand pointo caado desu ka?"
2. You: "Hai." (Yes, I agree!)
3. You get a card.

It's the easiest and most rewarding activity I've experienced in Tokyo. And, now I'm addicted to these little reward cards. It doesn't matter if I'm at a *supaa* (supermarket) or *depaato* (department store) or donut shop, I will always answer "Hai" to the question that ends with "....pointo caado desu ka?" But not only that, I now hoard and value my point cards like a 10-year old with his Pokemon deck. "Mister Donut-san, I choose you!"

"Do you even know how to figure out how many points you have on the cards?" my husband asked me.

"No," I said.

"Do you know how to redeem your points?"

"No," I said.

"Do you know what prizes you could earn with the points?"

"No," I said.

"You're just excited to communicate successfully in Japanese, right?"

"Hai," I said.

To be honest, in the past I have tried "*mo ichido onegaishimasu*" (one more time, please) and "*yukkuri kudasai*" (slowly, please) to the clerks, but answering with "*Hai*" is so much easier to say....and I know if I play my cards right one of these days I just might get a cool prize.

I have my eye on a Hello Kitty.

movie night

"Sna-ko fly-to?" my teenage son read as he translated the title very slowly.

"Sna-ko fly-to?" I repeated as I studied the DVD cover with him. "Sna-ko fly-to?" What is this movie?

After getting some language skills under our belt, my family and I decided it was time to join our neighborhood video store. With a Japanese DVD player (which we now have), logic skills to figure out the plugs, remote control and buttons (which my husband has) and the correctly formatted DVD (which this store has), we can now rent American movies.

But first, we have to figure out the movies.

After graciously volunteering (i.e. we lost to a family game of *Rock, Paper, Scissors*) for the maiden journey to the video store, my oldest son and I were now staring at the DVD covers. We were trying to figure out the movie based on the DVD cover. What is this movie? C'mon, observation skills.

Clue #1: Samuel L. Jackson
Clue #2: picture of an airplane
Clue #3: "Snako flighto. Snako flighto!" my son yelled as he reviewed the

Japanese title again. "Mom, don't you get it? 'Sna-ko Fly-to' means 'Snake Flight'. 'Snake Flight' must mean 'Snakes on a Plane.' This is the movie 'Snakes on a Plane!'"

"You're right!" I cheered as I gave him a fist pump. "Of course it is! Great job! OK. This is good. Now we know we are in the action aisle. However, we can't rent this movie for family night. Look! There's a cover with Matt Damon. Let's try to translate that one."

"I am pretty sure it's *Bourne* something," my son mumbled as he studied the Japanese writing.

"Good enough," I said as I put the DVD in my hand basket.

Thanks to my son's translating skills and Samuel L. Jackson, Matt Damon and Bruce Willis, we discovered the action aisle. From DVD covers with Will Ferrell and Jim Carrey, we determined the comedy corner. And, from DVDs of Kiefer Sutherland and *Lost*, we figured out the TV series shelves.

And, after a few minutes of attentive investigating, I found out that the section labeled "Hot! Hot! Hot!" in English referred to the newest DVD releases and not, well, not some other genre that would make a mommy blush.

"C'mon, Mom," my son whispered to me, "stop stalling. It's time to ask about becoming members. The clerk is staring at us."

"You ask how to join," I whispered back. "You know that you speak the best Japanese in the family. You know that the only phrase I can say well is *Toilet wa doko desu ka?*" (Where is the toilet?)

I'm really not sure how I did it; I just know that I refused to give up. Somehow we successfully became members of our local movie rental store; successfully rented movies; successfully watched the movies in English; returned them on time; and successfully learned the location of the nearest toilet.

It was a very successful mission, indeed.

Take that Jason Bourne!

miss pronunciation of tokyo

Yes, I'm on the lookout for a new hairdresser in Tokyo. This newest mission has nothing to do with my hair. It has absolutely everything to do with my pronunciation (mispronunciation) of Japanese words. I admit it. Despite my many attempts, I am consistently vexed by the vowel. I can't make sense of the short and long sounds.

When we first moved to Tokyo, I would always carry around a book of essential Japanese phrases which included such handy gems as:

Sumimasen (Excuse me. Sorry)
Eigo ga wakarimasu ka? (Do you understand English?)
Fohku o kudasai (Can I have a fork?)
Toilet wa doko desu ka? (Where is your toilet?)
Kore wa pen desu (This is a pen.)

But, now I've started carrying another book. A much more useful book. My little black notebook includes all the Japanese words that I've managed to mispronounce and should never, *ever* attempt to say again.

There was the time at a holiday dinner party when I mistakenly introduced my *shujin* (husband) as my *shuujin* (prisoner).

"I'm so sorry, Honey," I apologized to my husband after I was corrected by a Japanese friend.

"No problem, Warden," he said. "I think I got 20 years to life, but I'm hoping you will let me out early for good behavior."

And then, of course, there was that very embarrassing luncheon with my Japanese teacher and her friends when I thought I was explaining my enthusiasm for our new Japanese microwave. In actuality, I was praising my husband's genitals. I am still apologizing.

"Smooth, Mom, real smooth," my son whispered to me the other day, as he shook his head. "You just told that mother that her baby is scary-looking."

And, I have become notorious for complimenting mothers on their frightful-looking infants. My *kawaii* (cute) always sounds like *kowai* (scary), not matter how high pitched and excitedly I say it.

And, now, the newest nemesis to add to the list:

"*Byoin*," my sensei patiently repeated. "This is the word for hospital."

"Beyooeen?" I said.

"You just said *biyooin*. That is the word for hair dresser," my sensei explained. "Try again. *Byoin*."

"Bee yooo en. Bee you in. Bee yon. Beyonce," I said to my husband later that evening. "Let's just face facts. It's no use. It doesn't matter how much I try. I can't master the pronunciation."

I know. I know. It is bound to happen. Inevitably, I will confuse *byoin* and *biyooin*. I will end up taking a taxi to a stylist to perm a broken ankle or, perhaps much worse, I will show up in the emergency room for a case of the bad hair day.

So, in order to avoid being crowned Miss Pronunciation of Tokyo, I have decided to take some precautionary steps to limit my mistakes:

1. The one and only time I will say *kawaii* is during Halloween.
2. At my next formal gathering with my sensei and her friends, I will wear one of those disposable medical flu masks—but not out of courtesy to avoid spreading or catching a cold (the usual reason to wear a mask in Japan). I would wear it simply to remind myself to keep my mouth shut thus preventing any embarrassing communication gaffes.
3. I will find a new hairdresser. This is the only solution. I don't care how much the stylist costs, how far away the shop is, or even if the stylist can speak English. I don't even care if the shop has a working toilet or a pen. My only requirement is that it's located next to a hospital.

Of course, I have to say, being misunderstood sometimes has its surprise advantages. The other night at a restaurant, I was practicing my Japanese and called my husband by his Japanese name. All of a sudden, our waiter immediately rushed off. He returned a few minutes later with a pint.

My husband started to laugh. "The waiter heard you call me *Biru* and thought you were ordering a *biiru*."

In Japanese, my husband's name sounds like the word for *beer*?

Maybe I will accept the crown for Miss Pronunciation of Tokyo after all.

mind your please and queues

I have decided that it's time to embrace queues. When we first moved to Japan, I did whatever I could to *avoid* the unbelievable crowds and long lines.

If the line was too long to exit a train station, I would turn right around and get back on the train.

"Don't worry," I said to my kids, "the Yamanote train travels in a loop. We'll back here in 30 minutes."

When I felt intimidated by the mass of humanity crossing the streets at the busy Shibuya crossing, I just stayed put. "You go," I said to my husband. "I'll just stay here and keep Hachiko the dog company. You would like that, wouldn't you, doggy? Let me scratch you behind your ears."

"You know that I know that Hachiko is a dog statue, right?" my husband said.

But now...now I've come to realize that a line in Tokyo offers adventures. Each line tells a story. The line could lead to a warm donut. The line could lead to an exciting store opening. The line is a Tokyo experience not to be missed. Not to mention, queuing is easy.

1. Walk to your nearest queue.
2. Wait in the queue.
3. When you reach the front, say "*onegaishimasu*" (please). That's it.

Since I started lining up:

I've received free soap samples.
I've eaten a bowl of cold noodles.
I've watched cute puppies get shampooed.
I won a New Year's Day lucky bag.
I discovered a tiny bagel shop.
I got concert tickets.
I rode an exciting roller coaster at an amusement park.

I went to the rest room, even when I didn't have to go.
I (nearly) got a rabies shot.

I love Tokyo queuing. I love the order. I love the calm. I love the anticipation. I really love the surprise reward for patience.

And, so this morning, full of confidence and sense of adventure, I did it again. I saw a queue near my apartment, I waited in the queue, and I said *onegaishimasu* when I reached the front.

And, this is when I learned that sometimes the queue may actually lead you onto a bus.

"*Sumimasen.* Excuse me," I quietly whispered to another rider. "Do you speak English? What did the bus driver just say to me?"

"He said you packed lightly for a day at the mountains."

In Tokyo, every line tells a story. And, this one is telling me to be more careful about my please and queues. I promise that I will do just that, as soon as I find my way home.

face reading

"So, how do I look?" I asked my sons the other morning. I had spent some extra time on my appearance and was actually looking for honest feedback. "Do you see wrinkles and laugh lines? Do I look youthful and energetic? What is my best side? Left or right? Can you guess my demographic? Do I look thirsty?"

"I don't get it, Mom. Are you going out?" my youngest son asked me.

"Yes, in fact I am." I said. "I have a date with destiny."

"Who's Destiny? Does Dad know about this?" my youngest son asked.

"Daaaaaaad!"

Shoulders back.

Chin up.

No, wait. Chin down.

No, chin up.

Turn head left.

No, wait. Turn head right.

Glasses on.

No, wait. Glasses off.

Today I decided to check out the new beverage vending machine in Shinagawa Station, a major train station in Tokyo. During my time in Japan, I have seen and purchased from a variety of vending machines: machines with cold beverages; machines with hot beverages; and machines with both hot and cold beverages (a price in red means a hot drink; a blue price means cold). I have seen vending machines with beer, with energy drinks, with ice cream, with underwear. I have seen small machines, large machines, money machines, charge machines. I have seen machines with snacks; with tickets for noodles; and with kid toys. I had seen machines for photos, pachinko and parking. I had thought I had seen them all. But I had never seen a vending machine like this.

"Please no coffee, please no coffee, please no coffee," I muttered to myself as I posed in front of the new machine. I just didn't want a machine confirming that I looked tired.

Yes, there is a new beverage vending machine in town. Not only does it have a high-tech touch screen menu, but it also has a built-in camera. It reads your face and then highlights recommended drinks, based on your profile.

Flash.

"Please no coffee, please no coffee, please no coffee," I quietly chanted.

The first highlighted drink based on my profile: Water. No surprise there.

"Please no coffee, please no coffee, please no coffee," I chanted again.

I recognized the second recommended drink as green tea. Again, no surprise. Green tea is a very popular drink in Japan.

"Please no coffee. Please no coffee. Please no coffee," I chanted again as I waited for the third and final personal recommendation. This is it.

"So, Mom, how did it go with destiny?" my son asked when I returned home.

"Apparently, vitamin-enriched lemon liquid is written all over my face," I answered.

"Did you try it, Mom?" he asked. "Did you like it?"

"Well," I said as I looked over the small bottle. "The machine studied my face, right? So, the more I think about it; the more I am unsure if I am supposed to drink it...or wash my face with it."

not soccer mom, sumo mom

"Mom," my youngest son said to me about a month ago. "I want to sumo wrestle."

This request did not surprise me. My sons are always making interesting requests, such as:

"Mom, I want a clone."

"Mom, I want a lizard and I want to name it after you."

"Mom, I want a new chocolate ice cream cone. Mine just melted on the backseat of your car."

Not soccer mom, sumo mom **155**

Another reason why I wasn't surprised: we live in Japan now and Sumo is the national sport. Not to mention that my sons have been sumo wrestling in the living room ever since we moved in.

"What have you done to my rug?" I asked.

"C'mon, Mom, it's not a rug. It's a wrestling ring."

"Mom! Mom! Guess what?" My son said to me a few weeks ago. "I made it! I'm going to the tournament!" Sure enough, he had met the very strict criteria for an invitation to the youth sumo tournament:

He had attended every practice.

He attended practice with a good attitude.

He demonstrated sportsmanship.

He showed promising sumo skills and focus.

And, he had promised the coach I could get him to the tournament by 7:30 in the morning.

"7:30! 7:30 AM!" I said. "Don't sumo wrestlers sleep in on the weekends? I thought they wrestled in the afternoons?"

And, so there we were, early Sunday morning for the annual youth sumo tournament.

"You're next!" the coach told my son. "It's time to think of your move." (In hindsight, instead of focusing on his own move, it would have been better for my son to focus on his opponent's move which was basically to plow his head into my son and push him over the edge of the ring.)

"It's OK," my son's teacher said when my son lost. "It's double elimination. You're still in it."

Admittedly, I am not what you call a passionate sports fan. When my sons play, I happily bring sliced oranges for snack, I excitedly cheer from the stands, I am a very loyal customer at the Booster Club table. Just don't expect me to follow the goals, quarters, downs, and ups. In my world, everyone's a winner.

But now it is different. In America, I may have been a subdued soccer mom, but in Tokyo, I'm sumo mom.

"You know what this means," I said to my son. "This means it's comeback time. It's time to study other matches. It's time to focus on the moves. It's time to clear your mind. It's time to work on the intense eye stare. It's time to practice sweeping the leg."

My son started to walk away.

"Hey, where are you going?" I asked.

"To the concession stand," he said. "It's time to eat."

I started to give him the intense eye stare.

"Don't worry, Mom," he said. "Winning the sumo match is also part mind game. And, my mind is made up to win."

And he did win. When it was his turn to wrestle again, he won. One match after another match after another. And, he actually had a signature move: to grab his opponent's *mowashi* (the belt), dance around the ring a bit and then fling his opponent to the ground (affectionately referred to later as "the atomic wedgie.")

"Mom, Mom, I got a silver medal! I got second place!" A silver medal! Second place in a sumo tournament? Wow! Wow! WOW. The last time my youngest son won anything sports-related was in kindergarten. He won the Donut Eating Contest. And the prize was a glass of milk.

"C'mon, Mom," my son said. "You make it sound like it was easy. It wasn't easy. The donuts weren't just sitting on the table. They were hanging on a string."

the ticket to sleep

This is a first.

A definite first.

"See?" I said to the person sitting next to me on the train. "See that guy over there? He fell asleep standing up."

I didn't wait for my train buddy to answer.

"I call that the *Statue* style."

Ever since moving to Tokyo, I have observed hundreds and hundreds of passengers asleep on the train; not to mention, a variety of very impressive subway sleeping postures.

"See her?" I gently nudged my buddy. "Hands folded across lap. Head tilted way back. She's definitely what I call the *Stargazer*."

"And, that guy," I said as I viewed a snoring young man slouched in his seat with his hat pulled over his face. "His sleeping posture is what I call *The Cowboy*."

"And," I continued, "Do you see the woman who has fallen asleep with her head forward and her hands under her chin? She is *The Thinker*. And, that guy over there? He fell asleep with his sunglasses on. He is *The Poker Player*. But, to be honest with you, with the sunglasses, I truly can't tell. He actually could be a poker player."

"And," I continued, "Do you see the sleepy passenger whose head bobs side to side? He has definitely fallen asleep in *Table Tennis* mode."

"And, you," I said a bit louder to the person next to me. "You are what I call *The Trapper*."

This is a first.

A definite first.

My fellow train passenger had fallen asleep on my left shoulder. He was deeply asleep and comfortably snuggled.

I could not wake him with my silly subway sleep observations. "*Sumimasen, sumimasen*," I said a bit louder. "Ummm…my stop is coming up next….*sumimasen*…excuse me…."

I could not wake him with *sumimasen*.

"Hi, Honey," I pretended to speak on my cell phone (a Tokyo train taboo). "Mommy will be late tonight. MOMMY IS TRAPPED."

I could not wake him with a loud cell phone conversation.

This is a first.

A definite first.

Apparently, I have no choice. My solution may be a bit desperate and perhaps a bit unorthodox, but I have to get off the train. My stop is next. I have no choice. To quickly free myself from his resting head, maneuver around the other passengers and get out of the train door before it closes, I will need to perform a somewhat advanced calisthenics routine. A downward shoulder shrug and tuck and roll followed by a back handspring, aerial cartwheel and a stag leap should do it. I really wish I had some rhythmic gymnastic ribbons in my handbag to help stick the finish. Actually, I really wish I knew gymnastics.

"I have never understood how passengers can sleep on the subway," I yawned. "First, there's the repetitive mechanical sound…and then, all those announcements every few moments…kind of like white noise...surprisingly soothing...oops, there goes my stop...I'll get off at the next one...and, let's not forget about the complete passenger silence and the rumbling, the gentle rumbling and rocking…and the …and…the….hypnotic hum…"

This is a first.

A definite first.

ZZZZZZZ.

the wannabe crooner

From now on, I'm going with *genki*. After trying numerous Japanese language classes, CDs, and books, my brain has proven to be impervious to the Japanese language. So instead of struggling through my limited sentences, such as, "The weather is nice today, isn't it?" I have decided to just go with *genki* (I'm enthusiastic!)—it's simple, it's upbeat, it's lively, it's easy to see, it's agreeable. It's genki.

So, when a friend of mine recently invited my husband and me to karaoke, I answered with a very excited "genki."

"By the way," I said to my friend. "I'm not what you call a good singer."

"C'mon," she said. "Everybody is a good singer at karaoke."

I'm what you call a wannabe crooner. I love songs. I love listening to songs. I love to sing. I love to sing in the shower. I love to sing while making dinner. I love to sing while exercising.

"Honey, are you OK?" my startled husband asked me the other day in the fitness gym.

"Fine," I answered as I took off my headphones. "Why?"

"Oh," he answered. "You were making that noise. I thought you were in pain. I thought you were in labor which didn't make sense at all."

I'm a wannabe crooner. And if there was ever a time to rock out, this was it. So, I did. I chose my favorite song. I stood on the karaoke stage. I sang my heart out. I even ended my set with an awesome air guitar power stance.

However, apparently, even at karaoke, there are some singing standards. Because after my performance, the karaoke manager turned off my mike and handed me a tambourine.

I may be a wannabe crooner but, apparently, I should stick to back-up percussion.

the hai and bye

The waitress looked at me.

I looked at my husband.

My husband looked at me.

We looked at the waitress.

Although my husband and I have some Japanese language skills, we did not understand a word of what she had said to us.

At anxious moments like this, I start to panic. I know I should say something, but what? Quickly I thought of my options.

"*Moo ichido onegaishimasu.*" (One more time, please.) This is the ideal response. It is polite. It is relatively easy to say. However, I have had very little success with this phrase so far. For me, *moo ichido* actually brings me mo' trouble. I am implying that with a bit more focus I will understand the next time around or the time after that. Not going to happen. I always end up pantomiming. Or, I just bow and back away. Just bow and back away.

"Ashita wa ka-yoobi desu." (Tomorrow is Tuesday.) According to my sensei, this statement is my best Japanese sentence. It is clear. It is well pronounced. It makes sense. To tell you the truth, at first I was thrilled. Very thrilled. I have a best sentence! But soon I realized my best Japanese sentence is quite useless. First, it states the obvious. Second, I can only use it on Mondays.

"Kore wa pen desu." (This is a pen.) I like this sentence. You can say it anytime and just about anywhere. I can also describe the pen as small, blue, cute, interesting, performs well and belongs to me. Unfortunately, pen conversations are usually not conversation-starters, but conversation-enders.

"With a little milk and sugar, thanks." OK. I admit it. Out of desperation to say anything, I have sometimes just answered with this English line. Granted it is not very helpful at the gas station or at the post office, but, frequently, I do get a cup of coffee with a little milk and sugar that settles my nerves. Then, I can usually muster up a comment on today's nice weather. I'm pretty sure the post office personnel think I'm a high-strung meteorologist.

I looked at the waitress.

The waitress looked at me.

I looked at my pen. And, just when I thought it was time to show off my cute, small, interesting writing pen, I heard my husband say *"Hai"* (I agree).

"You understood what the waitress said?" I asked in disbelief.

"No idea," he admitted, "but from the context of the situation, I knew she had to be asking if we wanted our bill or if we wanted to bring home the leftovers. The context is the key."

He said "Hai." We paid the bill. We said "Bye" and we left. No drama. Just Hai and Bye.

Simple. Easy. Conversational. Agreeable. A bit adventurous. I love it.

"*Hai*. Bye," I replied to a clerk at a favorite store who then quickly presented me with a store loyalty point card.

"Hai. Bye," I answered to the barista at my local coffee shop who then wrapped up a cookie for me to take home.

"*Hai*," I cheerfully agreed with my new hairdresser. Before I had a chance to say "Bye," she unexpectedly cut several inches of my curly hair and started to chemically straighten it.

Sometimes *Hai* and *Bye* can be a *Hai* and *Sigh*.

sounds fishy

Act as a local tour guide for visiting guests? Yes, I can do that.

Wake up extremely early to wander in a fish market and watch a tuna auction? Yes, I can do that.

Try to speak and read a foreign language; eat a slippery bean breakfast called *natto*; "hunt and gather" around Tokyo for USA size 11 men's shoes; attempt to ride a *mamachan* bike with high heels; eat spicy ramen with chopsticks; push myself onto a crowded train....

Yes. Yes. Yes. I can do all that.

But fish food? Be fish food?

Slow down there, sister.

"What? What a minute. What are you talking about?" my friend said. "We are here because it was *your* idea, remember?"

Right. And, up to this point, my idea for a "new and exciting Tokyo adventure" was very sensible. And, an onsen spa park offered exactly the new adventure I was looking for: an opportunity to stroll through a

recreated Edo period village; eat Japanese noodles while wearing a *yukata* (a casual cotton kimono); enjoy stunning indoor and outdoor hot spring baths; walk through an open-air footbath; not to mention, experience a special and unique pedicure treatment called Doctor Fish.

By the way, note for next time: Doctor Fish is not a professional pedicurist with an intriguing surname.

Doctor Fish is actually a pool of carp that may or may not have a medical degree.

However, as my friend and I can attest, they do have an appetite. An appetite for dry epidermis.

"So," my friend said. "Let me get this straight? We sit down on the edge of the bath and put our feet in the water, so the fish can bite off the dry skin?"

"To be honest," I said as I stalled for time, "Sometimes I have wacky ideas. Let's see….there was the time I cooked a turkey with the giblets still inside to save time. Once I colored my hair Midnight Burgundy before heading off to college. A few years ago I went to a Halloween cocktail party dressed as a martini cocktail…I took the invitation too literally, I suppose,…another time…"

"You *have* to do it," my brave friend said as she plopped her feet into the pool of fish. "Remember, it was your idea."

"Don't look down. Don't look down. DON'T LOOK DOWN," I muttered to myself a few minutes later as I slowly lowered my feet into the fish footbath.

"Look up! Look up! LOOK UP!" the mass of fish seemed to gurgle as they vigorously swam to my feet and immediately swarmed my toes. "Glub. Glub. Glub. Ring the school bell, Finny, we have found ourselves in middle-aged dry epidermis heaven! C'mon, Bubbles, save some of that big toe for your father. Someone better ripple to Swimsy that Thanksgiving has come 'round again!"

Try to speak and read a foreign language? Yes, I can do that.

Calmly join three million commuters traveling through Shinjuku Station? Yes, I can do that.

Pantomime my grocery list; accept tissue packets from strangers; learn to correctly cover my wet umbrella in a plastic bag; mistakenly put a make up hood on my feet....

Yes. Yes. Yes. I can do all that.

But fish food? Be fish food for 15 minutes?

And, end up with unbelievable, amazing baby-smooth feet?

Yes, I can do that too.

"I got another idea," I said to my friend as we marveled at our soft feet, "Next time we come here, let's bring sushi. That way, we can nibble on sushi while the fish nibble us. What do you think?"

Like I said—sometimes I have wacky ideas.

trash talkin'

"Honey, I'm home," I cheerfully sang to my husband as I walked into the kitchen.

"I know," he said. "I heard you crinkling all the way down the hallway." Oh yes. There is no doubt. I crinkle.

I crinkle, crackle, crumple, rumple, wrinkle, ruffle, rustle, scrunch, crunch, swish and sometimes fizz.

This noisy career started quite innocently enough. During a tour of Tokyo with my relocation coordinator a while back, I naively asked if we could stop for a cup of coffee. I desperately needed my cup of jetlag java.

Instinctively, I took my coffee to the door and walked outside the café.

Instinctively, my relocation agent took her coffee to a table inside the cafe.

With confused expressions, we both stared at each through the store window.

"I know I'm acting a bit like a zombie due to the jet lag. But I can walk *and* drink coffee at the same time," I explained to my agent through the window. I waved to her palm-up to come out.

"It is better if we finish our drinks here," she said matter-of-factly. She waved to me palm-down to come in. Quickly.

As I watched other customers, I noticed that no one was taking their joe on-the-go. Right. The rationale must be cultural—perhaps drinking (and eating) while walking outside is considered ill-mannered here?

However, I soon discovered there was also a practical reason to avoid take-away—not only are the streets meticulously clean, but public trashcans are very difficult to find. For me, the solution to dealing with the inevitable trash collected from my errands and outings is simply, well, my pockets.

"Honey, I'm home," I loudly announced the other afternoon.

"How was your day?" my son asked.

"Well, I've got a pocketful of posies...plus...the morning paper, a coffee cup, multiple receipts, onigiri wrapper, bento box, empty water bottle, telephone bill receipt, newspaper, pocket-sized tissue packets, a rubber tree, a coat rack, a rabbit in a top hat..."

"Daaaad! Mom's talking trash again!"

Oh yes. There is no doubt. While living in Tokyo, I'll be the one loving the adventures, wearing the cargo pants and making some noise.

high time for high heels

I admit it. I have started to accept street handouts. Well, not exactly just any street handout. I absolutely love the free mini packets of facial tissues that Japanese company representatives hand out on the city streets. It's a wonderful, practical, packable, disposable, not to mention, soft and absorbent custom.

And, I admit it. Now, I've got quite a collection. I've got tissues in my purse, in my dog bag, in my earthquake kit, in my kids' school backpacks, in my husband's briefcase, in my pockets, in my hand, up my sleeve, in my grocery bags, and tucked in my umbrella.

I admit it. I have so many tissue packets now that I've started to pass them out on the street corner. "It's a great way to meet people," I said to my sons one busy afternoon in Shibuya. "Although I do seem to have a large number of new friends with allergies."

And, yes, I admit it. I also have footwear envy.

"Did you see that?" I asked one of my new allergic friends the other day. "I can't believe it! I have a hard time talking on my cell phone while walking. Did you see that woman? She was biking while talking on her cell phone, while holding an umbrella."

My friend sneezed.

"And you know the kicker?" I said. "She was also wearing high heels."

Oh, the heels. The heels. Tokyo women wear the most gorgeous, stylish, strappy, sexy high heel shoes. I see their pumps and mules and slingbacks stride around everyday and everywhere: up and down subway stairs, in and out of trains, back and forth for badminton and even hiking up a mountain.

"What are you doing, Mom?" my son asked me this morning.

"I decided it's high time for high heels," I said as I tried shoving my wide foot into my new city heels. "I decided (grunt, groan) it's time to kick off my moldable, cushioned, climate controlled, antibacterial sneakers and wiggle into the wedge. If I can fit my feet into some city heels (grunt, groan) then maybe I might fit in even better to Tokyo life."

"Mom," my son said with alarm as he stared at my foot. "I think your city heels are making your little toe bleed."

"Not to worry," I said. "I've got plenty of tissues."

the lunch date

"I don't know what to do," I said to my husband this morning. "What do you think?"

"What do you mean?" he asked. "Do you want to say no?"

No? No? I couldn't say no. How could I say no? This was an opportunity of a lifetime. Today, I was going out for lunch. And, it wasn't just any lunch. It was lunch at a Tokyo restaurant. And, it wasn't just any Tokyo restaurant.

"This is not just any Tokyo restaurant," the magazine editor had reminded me a few days before. "This restaurant has a two month waiting list for lunch. And, we would like you to come check it out and write a review for our English readers."

"It has a two month waiting list, remember?" I yelled to my husband from inside my closet. "What do you think I should wear? Aren't restaurant reviewers supposed to dress in a classy burgundy sports coat and black merino wool turtlenecks?"

After finally settling on my first restaurant review outfit: a maroon sweater and elastic-waist band black pants (It was an all-you-can-eat buffet after all), I decided I needed to focus on something even more important to help

prepare for my critique. I needed to do something about my name. This is Tokyo. I needed a new name that sounds sophisticated. I needed a name that sounds cultured and culinary. I got it.

"I thought of my restaurant review name," I said to my husband before he left for work. "Please refer to me as Francesca Fromage."

"Francesca Fromage," he said. "I think you just burned your breakfast in the toaster."

"So, what do you think?" the restaurant's public relations person asked me as I was sampling the coffee. I had taken the subway and easily found the restaurant. I had queued in the foyer. I had toured the dining room. I had stood in the buffet line. I had met the chefs. I had admired the setting. I had taken notes. I had sampled food. I had nibbled. I had dipped, sipped, sliced, diced. But, I had not quite finished testing the all-you-can-eat dessert station. There were so many desserts to select from: cakes, pastries, specialty breads, eclairs and even a very tempting display case of delicous-looking cookies with a sign that read in English "For display only. Do not eat."

"You know," I said. "I do feel a compliment coming. I really do. But, you know what would help? Another eclair. They are just so small, I couldn't quite savor it long enough to find the right word. Actually, maybe two or three more eclairs would help keep those compliments coming...maybe just the whole platter...."

I don't know if I'll write any more restaurant reviews. I don't know if I will be asked back to this restaurant. I don't know if I will write another article for this magazine. But, I do know that Francesca Fromage loves her chocolate.

dude hat

"Aah!" I heard my son scream from behind the apartment door. "A stranger is trying to get into the apartment! It's some kind of horrifying scarecrow in a dressy white belly shirt."

"I'm not a stranger," I said through the door. "I'm your mother. Please open the door. I can't reach the handle. Quickly! This shirt is cutting off the circulation of my neck and arms."

"Mom?" he questioned as he spied me through the security peep hole. "You tried to buy fancy clothes in Japan again, didn't you?"

"It said M size," I defended myself. "I thought M meant *medium*, not *microscopic*."

I know. I know. I know. I should have known better. As an American-sized, mature woman, I know it might be difficult—or impossible—for me to find designer apparel in my size (or the size I want to be) in Tokyo.

So, I'm stuck. I'm really stuck.

"I'm stuck!" I yelled at my son through the door. "Please open the door for Mommy. OK, you're right. I did it. I put on a dressy shirt that was too small for me. The collar is choking me. I need you to cut it off."

"C'mon, Mom!" my son said. "Not again!"

I know. I know. I know. I should have known better. In fact, when we first moved here, I immediately learned it might be challenging to clothes shop. "I'm looking for a fancy dress for an event," I had said to some other foreign mothers at the bus stop. "Does anyone know where I could buy one?"

My Japanese neighbor helpfully recommended a maternity store.

I was not expecting. And, I was not expecting that suggestion.

I know. I know. I know. I should have known better. But this is Tokyo and I had to test fashion fate once more. And, as soon as I pulled the dressy white shirt over my broad shoulders, it got stuck. "I love it," I barely whispered to the saleslady at the counter. "I love it so much that I will wear it just like this. Don't mind my tears. Tears of joy, really. By the way, I can't seem to turn my head or move my arms. Can you please just swivel me towards the door? *Doomo.*"

I know. I know. I know. I should have known better. So, that's why, I have decided that while living here I will only shop for hats.

1. A hat keeps your head warm.
2. A Tokyo hat is very chic and makes a fashion statement.
3. A hat transforms a plain outfit into a wow outfit.
4. A hat hides a bad hair day.
5. A hat is one size fits all.

"This hat," I said to my teenage son as we walked together to the train station. "It is not just a simple gray knit hat. It is a symbolic hat. I confidently walked down a random street in a foreign city. I discovered a new store. I found this great hat. I did this by myself. This hat is symbolic of progress, success and settling in. Enjoying a new culture is all about having the right *hatitude*."

"Well, it is certainly a popular hat, no doubt about that," my son said as we stood on the subway platform.

"Yes, we all have journeyed from clueless to genki," I continued. "We are all more comfortable and less anxious. We are all at ease with the cultural differences. And, along the way, I have even improved my fashion sense. Look at me, son. Take a good look at this hat. This is a great life lesson. I may be a fish out of water in Japan. But I am an adventurous, appreciative, confident fish in a stylish hat."

"I can't look at the you, Mom," my teenage son said as he averted his eyes. "Look around. Haven't you noticed that only men are wearing that style hat? Mom, I hate to tell you this, but you are wearing a man's hat. A DUDE HAT, Mom! You bought yourself a dude hat!"

"That's just ridiculous," I said as I fiddled with my new hat. "I am not wearing a man's hat. I wouldn't walk around town wearing a man's hat. This is NOT a man's hat. And, I will prove it to you, too. See that guy over there? I will ask him if this is a man's hat."

"Excuse me..." I asked a stylish Japanese man who was also waiting for the train. "Do you speak English?"

"Yes, sir," the Japanese man said to me, "I speak a little English."

I know. I know. I know. I should have known better. So, that's why, starting right now, I have decided that while living in Japan I will try to resist shopping for dressy shirts, formal dresses, heeled shoes or hats.

I'm sticking with scarves.

Let's be clear: a lady's scarf, that is.

Sumimasen, a sense of adventure, a sense of humor and a stylish scarf make one genki traveler in Japan.

Glossary

Arigato gozaimashita (a-ree-gah-to go-za-ee-mahsh-ta). This phrase is the past tense of "thank you very much." Say this polite expression after a transaction or to show your appreciation; for example, when someone shows you how to find your way back home.

Beef tongue (yes, beef tongue!). An entree like no other. The tongue of a cow can be boiled, broiled, pickled, stewed, grilled or sauteed. I served it frozen to the back of my freezer.

Biyooin (be-yo-eeen). This is the word for "hairdresser." However, due to a very similar pronunciation to the word for "hospital," (see below) you may discover yourself at the emergency room for a bad hair day.

Byooin (be-yo-een). This word for "hospital" has a critical pronunciation distinction from the word for "hairdresser." Just don't ask me what it is.

Depaato (day-pah-toe). Service, sights and smells, oh my! Be prepared to be amazed. The depaato is an impressive multi-floor experience. Step into a world of impeccably-suited and extremely cheerful sales clerks, efficient "elevator ladies," artfully displayed merchandise, unbelievable quality, and perfectly-wrapped gifts. Does shopping make you hungry? No worries—just head up to the restaurants on the top floor or down to the food floor in the basement. My tip for shoppers: doors open at 10 AM. My tip for nonshoppers: depaatos are perfect city landmarks.

Domo (dough-moe). Depending on the situation, domo can mean "sorry," "hello," (a casual) "thank you" or even "very much." It is an easy-to-say, helpful, ambiguous expression, thus perfect for foreigners. Domo for domo!

Genki (gang-key). When asked, "Ogenki desu ka?" ("How are you? Are you well?"), the standard reply is "Genki desu." ("I am well. I am in good spirits.") I love this word. Yes, I love it because it is easy to say, but also because it is more than just a customary answer—it is an attitude. To be "genki" is to be enthusiastic, fun, friendly and positive. A sense of adventure, sense of humor, stylish scarf and *sumimasen* are the keys to many genki Japan adventures.

Hai (hi). "Yes, OK, I agree." Disclaimer: because it is simple to say, it is very tempting to enthusiastically respond to Japanese questions with "hai" and unknowingly agree to an adventure, such as soaking naked in a hot tub with strangers. Sometimes, it is best to politely bow and back away. Bow and back away.

Hair & Make Shop. This is short for "hair and make up" shop which seem to be around every corner. The price usually includes a very relaxing, sleep-inducing head and neck massage. It is very cute when a toddler falls asleep during the massage; less so when a middle-aged mom nods off.

Hiragana (hee-rah-gah-na). Memorizing the 46 Hiragana characters is a good start to understanding written Japanese. Each character represents a syllable—so it is relatively easy to pick up. However, since written Japanese is actually a combination of Hiragana, Katakana and Kanji…well, good luck to you.

Hygiene Office. This is the name of the office where residents must register their dogs. It is a very serious office, so try not to snicker at the name.

Ichi, ni, san (ee-chee, nee, sahn). These words translate to the numbers "one, two, three." In Japan, quantity is expressed with numbers or counters. And there are different counters for different objects. For example, flat objects, appliances, small animals, bottles, and the number of people each have their own unique counter word. If all else fails, just use your fingers to point and count.

Irashaimasen (ear-rah-shy-ma-sen). This very cheerful, high-pitched expression means "welcome." You don't need to enthusiastically say anything back. And, as I found out, you don't need to take off your shoes.

Kanji (kahn-jee). Another written language in the Japanese alphabet. There are thousands of Kanji (Chinese characters) and many of these pictograms have two sounds and meanings. Beautiful? Yes. Intriguing? Yes. Fun? Yes. Complex? Yes.

Katakana (kah-tah-kah-nah). Another Japanese writing system. Katakana syllables have the same sounds as Hiragana, but are commonly used for foreign words. Helpful travelers tip: If you are in a pinch, just add "o" or "u" sound to an English word ("ticket-o," "gate-o," "orange juice-u," "soup-u"), it sometimes helps with communication.

Kawaii (ka-wa-eeeeeeee). Means adorable and perhaps frilly. Kawaii appears to include Hello Kitty merchandise, little dogs, babies, and cell phone accessories. Beginner Japanese speakers should be careful pronouncing this word because, if you aren't careful, *kawaii* can sound like *kowaii* (ko-wa-eee) which means "scary." And calling a baby *kowaii* is not *kawaii* at all.

Koko. This means "here." For instance, if you want a taxi driver to stop, say "Koko desu." The pronunciation is similar to the English word "cocoa", but believe me, they have very different meanings.

Kudasai (koo-da-sigh). This means "please." Please use it when making a request, such as "Taxi kudasai." A popular phrase to say and hear is *chotto matte kudasai* (cho-toe-ma-teh koo-da-sigh) which means "please wait a moment." A perfect phrase to say to stall for time as you try to figure out how to flush a toilet.

Make up hood. Found in depaato dressing rooms, this paper hoodie is to help protect new clothing from a customer's make up. It is not a puppet, a face cloth or an oversized dressing room slipper. Long story.

Midori no Hi (me-do-ree no-he). To my surprise, Green (*midori*) Day (*hi*) is not a translation for Green Day, the punk rock band. Green Day is a national holiday in the spring to celebrate and appreciate nature. If you go to the local ticket office and say "Midori no Hi," you will receive suggestions to stroll a garden, plant a tree, enjoy a picnic, travel, or clean up the local park, but you will not get five tickets to the upcoming rock concert.

Onegashimasu (oh-nee-gah-shee-ma-su). A more formal and polite "please" than *kudasai*. It is also tradition to say it to the bus driver. Please don't ask me why.

Onsen (ahn-sen). The hot spring bathing suit-less bath is a favorite cultural hobby. Yes, you will need to shed your clothes...and your inhibitions. It is a wonderful, relaxing, exhilerating experience. Travelers tip: when going to an onsen, be sure to stand tall and walk proud.

Pocari Sweat (poh-ka-ree sweat). A popular sports drink. It does not contain sweat. According to its label, Pocari Sweat "smoothly supplies the lost water and electrolytes during perspiration." Now, I get it.

Pointo caado (poi-n-toe cah-dough) Nearly every business offers point cards (loyalty cards) for discounts on future purchases. The only downside is that you might have to buy an extra large purse to carry all your point cards. Or a car.

Rice cooker. Convenient steamed cooker that cooks more than rice. You gotta get one.

Shujin (shoo-jean). The Japanese word for "husband."

Shuujin (shooo-jean). The Japanese word for "prisoner." Coincidence?

Slippers. Crucial footwear in Japan. BYOS. Travelers should pack your own slippers unless your shoe size is size 10 or smaller (men); or size 6 or smaller (women). Japanese homes, shrines and some restaurants require slippers instead of outdoor shoes. Also, for goodness sake, learn from me and always wear your good socks.

Sumimasen (soo-me-mah-sen). If you visit Japan and you can memorize only one word—this is it! It can mean "excuse me," "I'm sorry," and "thank you." I don't make any apologies that I use this word all the time. *Sumimasen!*

Sumo. Sumo wrestling is the national pastime. If possible, see a sumo wrestling match during your visit (tournaments in Tokyo are in January, May, and September). Be warned: you may quickly become addicted to this sport.

Taxi. Japanese taxis are immaculately clean from top to bottom, including white doilies on the seat head rests. Most taxis (pronounced "tax-shi" in Japanese) have

GPS systems; simply show the driver the exact address, a phone number or a landmark on the map and you are good to go. And there's more! No need to touch the door. Passenger doors are remotely opened and closed by the driver. Anything else? No tipping. Know the address, leave the door to the driver, don't tip, sit back and enjoy the ride.

Toire (toy-ray) or Toilet. If you visit Japan, memorize "Toire wa doko desu ka or Toilet wa doko desu ka?" (Where is your toilet?) Even if you don't have to go, you must check out the Japanese toilets because they are amazing thrones! Most feature a heated seat that quickly becomes your think tank as you ponder how to flush. Some play music or nature sounds to mask your natural sounds. Some have fans, massage streams, dry air...what are you waiting for? Go now.

Yonsen. "Yon" means "four." "Sen" means "thousand." So, "yonsen" means "four thousand." Easy, right? Except, if slightly mispronounced, it sounds like "onsen." Bank tellers may be very confused if you approach the desk asking to bathe naked. Consider writing the number down on a piece of paper instead.

Wakarimas (wah-kah-ree-mas). To understand. For instance, "Nihongo ga wakarimas ka?" means "Do you understand Japanese?" and "Eigo ga wakarimas ka?" means "Do you understand English?" If the answer is "Hai", great and congratulations. If the reply is a head shaking "no," well, you can always pantomime. The only words I won't pantomime: antacid, playground and bikini.

Wakarimasen (wah-kah-ree-ma-sen). "I do not understand." For example, "Sumimasen. Wakarimasen" would translate as "I don't have any idea what you are saying, give it up, lady. Just order your darn coffee in English."

Wakarimashita (wah-ka-ree-mash-ta). Translates as "I understood what you said." Really? You understood me? It's a miracle! I highly suggest having a victory dance move to celebrate a successful communication. I have one and that is probably why I usually shop alone.

Otsukaresamadeshita, readers!
Thank you for your fatigue!